PENGUIN BOOKS

PETER REDGROVE : POEMS 1954–1987

Peter Redgrove was born in 1932. He read Natural Sciences at Cambridge and was a scientific journalist and copywriter for some years. From 1962, for three years, he was Gregory Fellow in Poetry at Leeds University. In 1966 he became Resident Author at Falmouth School of Art, a position he held until 1983. During that time he was Visiting Professor at Colgate University in the United States. From 1985 to 1987 he was Leverhulme Emeritus Fellow. He was made a Fellow of the Royal Society of Literature in 1982.

Regarded as one of the country's leading poets, Peter Redgrove has won many prizes, including the 1977 Prudence Farmer Poetry Award and the 1985 Cholmondeley Award. His latest volumes of poetry include *The Man Named East*, *The Mudlark Poems and Grand Buveur* and *In the Hall of the Saurians*. His first novel, *In the Country of the Skin*, was widely praised and won the 1973 *Guardian* Fiction Prize. He has also written, with Penelope Shuttle, a documentary study of the human fertility cycle entitled *The Wise Wound* (1978, Penguin 1980, rev. edn 1986) and in 1987 published his second non-fiction book, *The Black Goddess and the Sixth Sense*. His plays have been broadcast on radio and television and include *Martyr of the Hives*, winner of the 1981 Giles Cooper Award, *Florent and the Tuxedo Millions*, winner of the 1982 Prix Italia, and the acclaimed Radio 3 season of plays from Grimm in 1987.

POEMS 1954–1987

PETER REDGROVE

PENGUIN BOOKS

PENGUIN BOOKS

Published by the Penguin Group
27 Wrights Lane, London w8 5TZ, England
Viking Penguin Inc., 40 West 23rd Street, New York, New York 10010, USA
Penguin Books Australia Ltd, Ringwood, Victoria, Australia
Penguin Books Canada Ltd, 2801 John Street, Markham, Ontario, Canada L3R 1B4
Penguin Books (NZ) Ltd, 182–190 Wairau Road, Auckland 10, New Zealand

Penguin Books Ltd, Registered Offices: Harmondsworth, Middlesex, England

First published in Great Britain as *The Moon Disposes: Poems 1954–87* by
Martin Secker & Warburg Ltd 1987
Published in Penguin Books, 1989

Printed and bound in Great Britain by
Cox & Wyman Ltd, Reading

CONTENTS

from THE MUDLARK POEMS & GRAND BUVEUR (1986)

from IN THE HALL OF THE SAURIANS (1987)

ACKNOWLEDGEMENTS

Acknowledgements are due to the following:

Fuller d'Arch Smith Ltd (for poems originally published in *The Hermaphrodite Album*); Rivelin Grapheme Press (for poems originally published in *The Mudlark Poems & Grand Buveur*); Routledge & Kegan Paul (for poems originally published in *The Collector, The Nature of Cold Weather, At the White Monument, The Force, Dr Faust's Sea-Spiral Spirit, Sons of My Skin, From Every Chink of the Ark, The Weddings at Nether Powers, The Apple-Broadcast* and *The Man Named East*).

AGAINST DEATH

We are glad to have birds in our roof
Sealed off from rooms by white ceiling,
And glad to glimpse them homing straight
Blinking across the upstairs windows,
And to listen to them scratching on the laths
As we bed and whisper staring at the ceiling.
We're glad to be hospitable to birds.
In our rooms, in general only humans come,
We keep no cats and dislike wet-mouthed dogs,
And wind comes up the floorboards in a gale,
So then we keep to bed: no more productive place
To spend a blustery winter evening and keep warm.
Occasionally a spider capsises in the bath,
Blot streaming with legs among the soap,
Cool and scab-bodied, soot-and-suet,
So we have to suffocate it down the pipe
For none of us'd have dealings with it,
Like kissing a corpse's lips, even
Through the fingers, so I flood it out.
In our high-headed rooms we're going to breed
Many human beings for their home
To fill the house with children and with life,
Running in service of the shrill white bodies,
With human life but for sparrows in the roof,
Wiping noses and cleaning up behind,
Slapping and sympathising, and catching glimpses
Of each other and ourselves as we were then,
And let out in the world a homing of adults.

And if there ever should be a corpse in the house
Hard on its bedsprings in a room upstairs,
Smelling of brass-polish, with sucked-in cheeks,
Staring through eyelids at a scratching ceiling,

Some firm'd hurry it outdoors and burn it quick –
We'd expect no more to happen to ourselves
Our children gradually foregoing grief of us
As the hot bodies of the sparrows increase each summer.

Swallowing earth through his nose,
The worm inches his miles;
The fine grain at the grassroots stirs
And his limy lips nibble in day –
Then, snap! like a gun, from the high air
The bird's tapping beak is in through the stalks
And worm hurried thro gh height that smarts his moist hide,
Rushes into his wounds: to the horrible children
That crash in the twisted nest. These birds
Hoist up the whorled Cellini snail,
Crazing him hak-hak on rocks.

Now why faze the innocent slowcoach worm,
The mother-o'pearl-boned, lip-skirted snail?
Worm's not lazy carrion! he skeins his toil-holes
Lined with worm-sweat. He eats what he finds:
Slides like a train through abominable patches
Or tugs in with all muscles the toothsome leaf.
Snail shaves his salads from stem and leaf.

It is lechery, lechery: fits and starts,
Grabbing and gluttony, while the sightless worm
Like soft successive links of a spring
Wants to pile out and slubber for hours
In the moist slow shade among the twigs
And damn the birds! in this slithing-time.

But if the air is clear, the trees are full;
Birds tread their birds with a hop-snap-tup
Bloody amid a mist of loose feathers – and, safe,
Snail pulls his skull over his ears, to a shriek.

LAZARUS AND THE SEA

The tide of my death came whispering like this
Soiling my body with its tireless voice.
I scented the antique moistures when they sharpened
The air of my room, made the rough wood of my bed (most
dear),
Standing out like roots in my tall grave.
They slopped in my mouth and entered my plaited blood
Quietened my jolting breath with a soft argument
Of such measured insistence, untied the great knot of my
heart.

They spread like whispered conversations
Through all the numbed rippling tissues radiated
Like a tree for thirty years from the still centre
Of my salt ovum. But this calm dissolution
Came after my agreement to the necessity of it;
Where before it was a storm over red fields
Pocked with the rain and the wheat furrowed
With wind, then it was the drifting of smoke
From a fire of the wood, damp with sweat,
Fallen in the storm.

I could say nothing of where I had been,
But I knew the soil in my limbs and the rain-water
In my mouth, knew the ground as a slow sea unstable
Like clouds and tolerating no organisation such as mine
In its throat of my grave. The knotted roots
Would have entered my nostrils and held me
By the armpits, woven a blanket for my cold body
Dead in the smell of wet earth, and raised me to the sky
For the sun in the slow dance of the seasons.
Many gods like me would be laid in the ground
Dissolve and be formed again in this pure night
Among the blessing of birds and the sifting water.

But where was the boatman and his gliding punt?
The judgment and the flames? These happenings
Were much spoken of in my childhood and the legends.
And what judgment tore me to life, uprooted me
Back to my old problems and to the family,
Charged me with unfitness for this holy simplicity?

OLD HOUSE

I lay in an agony of imagination as the wind
Limped up the stairs and puffed on the landings,
Snuffled through floorboards from the foundations,
Tottered, withdrew into flaws, and shook the house.
Peppery dust swarmed through all cracks,
The boiling air blew a dry spume from other mouths,
From other hides and function:
Scale of dead people fountained to the ceiling –
What sort of a house is this to bring children to,

Burn it down, build with new-fired brick;
How many times has this place been wound up
Around the offensive memories of a dead person,
Or a palette of sick colours dry on the body,
Or bare arms through a dank trapdoor to shut off water,
Or windows filmed over the white faces of children:
'This is no place to bring children to'

I cried in a nightmare of more
Creatures shelled in bone-white,
Or dead eyes fronting soft ermine faces,
Or mantled in carnation, dying kings of creation,
Or crimson mouth-skirts flashing as they pass:
What a world to bring new lives into,

Flat on my back in a warm bed as the house around me
Lived in the wind more than the people that built it;
It was bought with all our earned money,
With all the dust I was nearly flying from my body
That whipped in the wind in this normal November,
And outstretched beside her in my silly agony
She turned in her sleep and called for me,
Then taught me what children were to make a home for.

DEAD BIRD

Flies cauterise as they eat dabbing the parts
Making a warped map of our bird
Scab hillocks and the hard brume of weals,
Ochre bars and divots of gristle.
I shovel it off my lawn with a hoe,
I trowel a hole of centipedes and sand
Savages that now stray without thoughts
Through all the upstart galleries of that flier
Whose memory lies in feathers crinkling
Over the whole endeavour of our sun-dried lawn.

The father darts out on the stairs
To listen to that keening
In the upper room, for a change of note
That signifies distress, to scotch disaster,
The kettle humming in the room behind.

He thinks, on tiptoe, ears a-strain,
The cool dawn rising like the moon:
'Must not appear and pick him up;
He mustn't think he has me springing
To his beck and call,'
The kettle rattling behind the kitchen door.

He has him springing
A-quiver on the landing –
For a distress-note, a change of key,
To gallop up the stairs to him
To take him up, light as a violin,
And stroke his back until he smiles.
He sidles in the kitchen
And pours his tea . . .

And again stands hearkening
For milk cracking the lungs.
There's a little panting,
A cough: the thumb's in: he'll sleep,
The cup of tea cooling on the kitchen table.

Can he go in now to his chair and think
Of the miracle of breath, pick up a book,
Ready at all times to take it at a run
And intervene between him and disaster,
Sipping his cold tea as the sun comes up?

He returns to bed
And feels like something, with the door ajar,
Crouched in the bracken, alert, with big eyes
For the hunter, death, disaster.

FLIES

The small wind of a fly's wing stirs my thumb,
And rounds and stops, and bends a dog-eared paper,
And flies away upon a shadow, then pauses on a cloth,
Poses, a shabby, crooked, thin-shanked trumpeter
With comb-and-tissue-paper voice,
Small elephant on wings with dabbing trunk,
Almost a circus animal: think
Of him tamed with spangled side-cloths.
Comic, he keeps the seasons of the refuse-dump,
And clusters round the grimy housemaid as she throws it out,
And in the sun they leap upon each others' backs:
Fawning, predictable, that die in hordes,
Shun the rain, in winter live in caves,
Savage with no weapon but a voice,
Twitching, nervous, short-lived, suspicious,
Spry, lecherous, dirt-mouthed and golden-bodied,
They wash their paws and faces like any sleeking cat,
They fill the air in chase of livelihood,
They snuffle up the smells around dry bone.
I walk in leeward of a mound of dung,
They offer me a bouquet of high-pitched wings,
A tapered whirlwind of dirt and filmy lace.

Fine-grained eyes, hemispherical and dull,
From lakes of sewage bordered by dusty hills
You infect my meal with your self-interest
Steadfast in the light with dabbing trunks,
Infect my tender mouth with what I kiss.
What refuse of whose loves is my career,
Whose diseases must I take upon my back,
What silent lips and nostrils are your food,
Whose film-eyed ending is my start of pain?

THE COLLECTOR

Caught in a fold of living hills he failed,
For, out of his childhood, he had wandered on
An alien soil;
Extending his amiable senses, he found them blind.

The senses still, the reason kept its sway;
Nothing could be of conscious choice but still he chose
Observations made to stir him in default of love.
And thus the beauty and the terror of his life
Moved him mildly. This living landscape where before
He failed, was absorbing, with the horny rocks and the
Mist that glittered like a skin,
And with reasonable curiosity he saw
Crows fall from the sky, lilac tongues
Of death in the square-cut hedge; such omens
Were full of interest.

A busy life it was, watching the people with the
Gay clothes and the lives whipped like tops;
The tongued folk who burned with
The fire that warmed his watching.

At the end, as he would have wished, the Divine
Fingers plucked him from this skin
With much pain for both;
For he was interested in his illness,
And the world, strange to relate, had grown fond of him.

BEDTIME STORY
FOR MY SON

Where did the voice come from? I hunted through the rooms
For that small boy, that high, that head-voice,
The clatter as his heels caught on the door,
A shadow just caught moving through the door
Something like a school-satchel. My wife
Didn't seem afraid, even when it called for food
She smiled and turned her book and said:
'I couldn't go and love the empty air.'

We went to bed. Our dreams seemed full
Of boys in one or another guise, the paper-boy
Skidding along in grubby jeans, a music-lesson
She went out in the early afternoon to fetch a child from.
I pulled up from a pillow damp with heat
And saw her kissing hers, her legs were folded
Far away from mine. A pillow! It seemed
She couldn't love the empty air.

Perhaps, we thought, a child had come to grief
In some room in the old house we kept,
And listened if the noises came from some especial room,
And then we'd take the boards up and discover
A pile of dusty bones like charcoal twigs and give
The tiny-sounding ghost a proper resting-place
So that it need not wander in the empty air.

No blood-stained attic harboured the floating sounds,
We found they came in rooms that we'd warmed with our life.
We traced the voice and found where it mostly came
From just underneath both our skins, and not only
In the night-time either, but at the height of noon
And when we sat at meals alone. Plainly, this is how we found
That love pines loudly to go out to where
It need not spend itself on fancy and the empty air.

MEMORIAL

David Redgrove: 28 December 1937–24 December 1957

Two photographs stand on the dresser
Joined up the spine. Put away
They fold until they kiss each other,
But put out, they look across the room.
My brother and myself. He is flushed and pouting
With heart, and standing square,
I, already white-browed and balding,
Float there, it seems, and look away.
You could look at us and say I was the one of air,
And he the brother of earth
Who, in Christmas-time, fell to his death.

Fancy, yes; but if you'd seen him in his life
There'd be his bright blond hair, and that flush,
And the mouth always slightly open, and the strength
Of body: those muscles! swelled up with the hard
                              hand-springs at night
Certainly, but strong. I, on the other hand
Was remote, cross, and disengaged, a proper
Bastard to my brother, who enjoyed things,
Until he was able to defend himself. It's June;
Everything's come out in flush and white,
In ruff and sun, and tall green shoots
Hard with their sap. He's ashes
Like this cigarette I smoke into grey dryness.
I notice outside my window a tree of blossom,
Cherries, I think, one branch bending heavy
Into the grey road to its no advantage.
The hard stone scrapes the petals off,
And the dust enters the flower into its peak.

It is so heavy with flowers it bruises itself:
It has tripped, you might say, and fallen,
Cannot get up, so heavy with dust.
The air plays with it, and plays small-chess with the dust.

THE ARCHAEOLOGIST

So I take one of those thin plates
And fit it to a knuckled other,
Carefully, for it trembles on the edge of powder,
Restore the jaw and find the fangs their mates.

The thorny tree of which this is the gourd,
Outlasting centuries of grit and water,
Re-engineered by me, stands over there,
Stocky, peeling, crouched and dangling-pawed.

I roll the warm wax within my palm
And to the bone slowly mould a face
Of the jutting-jawed, hang-browed race;
On the brute strength I try to build up a calm,

For it is a woman, by the broad hips;
I give her a smooth skin, and make the mouth mild:
It is aeons since she saw her child
Spinning thin winds of gossamer from his lips.

WITHOUT EYES

Today, to begin with, she will do without eyes.

Staring at the speckled ruby eyelids make of the sunny window
Now she tries the world with her eyelids closed;
Pulls the length of her body out of the rasp of sheets
Into her self-made night-time; delicately shuffles her way
                                                   along the hairy carpet
To the cool rim she traces round with a finger.
Heaves the heavy bulging of the water-jug, tilts
And lets it grow lighter,
The tinkling in the bowl wax to a deep water-sound.
Sluices her bunched face with close hands, finds natural grease,
With clinking nails scrabbles for the body of the sprawling soap,
Rubs up the fine jumping lather that grips like a mask,
                                                   floods it off,
Solving the dingy tallow.
Bloods and plumps her cheeks in the springy towel, a
                                        rolling variable darkness
Dimpling the feminine fat-pockets under the deep coombs
                                             of bone
And the firm sheathed jellies above that make silent
                                     lightning in their bulbs.

Moves to her clothes – a carpet-edge snatches her toe
Plucking the tacks sharply like flower-stalks from the boards but
Leaves her smirking in darkness. Dresses:
Cupped hands grip. The bridge chafes quickly over the thighs
And closes on the saddled groin,
Her silk dress thunders over her head and on to the
                                        flounced opening

Into quiet
And her eyes clip open on the ardent oblivion of her
                                        resolution and
The streets and clouds from her high window, swimming
                                and dazzled, rush in.

GHOSTS

The terrace is said to be haunted.
By whom or what nobody knows; someone
Put away under the vines behind dusty glass
And rusty hinges staining the white-framed door
Like a nosebleed, locked; or a death in the pond
In three feet of water, a courageous breath?
It's haunted anyway, so nobody mends it
And the paving lies loose for the ants to crawl through
Weaving and clutching like animated thorns.
We walk on to it,
Like the bold lovers we are, ten years of marriage,
Tempting the ghosts out with our high spirits,
Footsteps doubled by the silence . . .

. . . and start up like ghosts ourselves
Flawed lank and drawn in the greenhouse glass:
She turns from that, and I sit down,
She tosses the dust with the toe of a shoe,
Sits on the pond's parapet and takes a swift look
At her shaking face in the clogged water,
Weeds in her hair; rises quickly and looks at me.
I shrug, and turn my palms out, begin
To feel the damp in my bones as I lever up
And step toward her with my hints of wrinkles,
Crows-feet and shadows. We leave arm in arm
Not a word said. The terrace is haunted,
Like many places with rough mirrors now,
By estrangement, if the daylight's strong.

TWO POEMS

I SPRING

To pass by a pondbrink
Trodden by horses
Where among the green horsetails
Even the hoofprints
Shiver with tadpoles
Comma'd with offspring
And moist buds flick awake
On breeze-floundering sallows.

II EPHEMERID

The fly is yellowed by the sun,
Her plating heaves, her wings hum,
Her eyes are cobbled like a road,
Her job is done, her eggs are stowed
No matter in what. The sun
Yellows the hemlock she sits upon;
Her death is near, her job is done,
Paddling in pollen and the sun,
She swings upon the white-flowered weed,
As a last duty, yellow with seed,
She falters round the flower-rim,
Falters around the flower-rim.

CORPOSANT

A ghost of a mouldy larder is one thing: whiskery bread,
Green threads, jet dots,
Milk scabbed, the bottles choked with wool,
Shrouded cheese, ebony eggs, soft tomatoes
Cascading through their splits,
Whitewashed all around, a chalky smell,
And these parts steam their breath. The other thing
Is that to it comes the woman walking backwards
With her empty lamp playing through the empty house,
Her light sliding through her steaming breath in prayer.

Why exorcise the harmless mouldy ghost
With embodied clergymen and scalding texts?
Because she rises shrieking from the bone-dry bath
With bubbling wrists, a lamp and steaming breath,
Stretching shadows in her rooms till daybreak
The rancid larder glimmering from her corpse
Tall and wreathed like moulds or mists,
Spoiling the market value of the house.

MORE LEAVES FROM
MY BESTIARY

I SPIDER

Now, the spires of a privet fork from the hedge
And stretch a web between them;
The spider-nub eases his grip a trifle, twists a thread safe,
And the afternoon is quiet again.

Damp clouds drift above him; a burst of rain
Runs him back along a vane
To a leaf-shed, while it beads his web
And raises weed-smells from below
Of vetch, fumitory, and small mallow.

Hanging there are a dozen or so
Brown shells which tremble.
The curtain is ripped from the sun, and grass again
Leaps into its fumble:

Ants totter with their medicine balls and cabers, stone walls
Pop with their crickets;
A bluefly, furry as a dog, squares up
To the web and takes it with a jump like a hoop

And spider springs round like a man darting
To the fringes of a dogfight;

Tugging like a frantic sailor, buzzing like a jerky sawyer,
Fly finishes in swaddling
Tight as a knot
From the spinnerets' glistening.

And though spider
Hangs a little lower than the sun
Over all their heads, all
Seem ignorant of that passing;
The afternoon, the ebullience increases
Among the low boughs of the weeds
And spider steady, like a lichened glove
Only a little lower than the sun; none
Takes account of that to and fro passing,
Or of the manner of that death in swaddling.

II BASILISK

Rising above the fringe of silvering leaves
A finger, tanned and scaly, gorgeous, decayed,
Points to the shivering clouds, then turns down
Most slowly, towards you. The light catches, cold and hard
Pulls round the polished bone of fingernail
Arrests attention, the prey falls dead.

Bone mirrors have the quickest way to die
The sunlight loses strength and sap drained
Out and lost, distils a beam of purest mortality
Set in the velvet sockets of a fabled bird.
A mandarin of birds, exalted, alone
Sweeping its cold avenue of dying trees
Its restlessness oppressed for new fuel, warm
And busy not to lift its eyes, unrealised sin
Committed out of favour, and it dies.

But when it dies the silks collapse and draw aside.
The idle naturalist to draw this legend to its wisest close,
Pries. The walking-stick at first disturbs a swarm
But no danger from the tawny ground, it lies
As still as where it dropped. Newspaper and a spade
A tin tray in the quietest room; probes,

Licks like an eagle with his sharpest knives.
Fat, flesh, yes, and normal bones
Sincerely documented, the head from behind now
The brain, enlarged, hard and crisp as ice
No poison, the smell of preservatives, the face
At last, nostrils and beak, a wrinkled neck,
The eyelids closed. He pulls these aside,
They rustle, a smell like pungent spice

He catches. How curious, the eyes as dead
And white as buttons, hard, adamantine, he tries
To scratch them with his knife, with no effect,
Revolves the problem in his clouding head.
Then the light catches, and he dies.

EXPECTANT FATHER

Final things walk home with me through Chiswick Park,
Too much death, disaster; this year
All the children play at cripples
And cough along with one foot in the gutter.
But now my staircase is a way to bed
And not the weary gulf she sprinted down for doorbells
So far gone on with the child a-thump inside;
A buffet through the air from the kitchen door that sticks
Awakes a thumb-size fly. Butting the rebutting window-pane
It shouts its buzz, so I fling the glass up, let it fly
Remembering as it skims to trees, too late to swat,
That flies are polio-whiskered to the brows
With breeding-muck, and home
On one per cent of everybody's children.

So it is the week when Matron curfews, with her cuffs,
And I draw back. My wife, round as a bell in bed, is white and
                                                         happy.
Left to myself I undress for the night
By the fine bright wires of lamps; hot tips
To burrowing cables, the bloodscheme of the house,
Where flame sleeps. That,
With a shallow on the mattress from last night,
Is enough to set me thinking on fired bones
And body-prints in the charcoal of a house, how
Darkness stands for death, and how afraid of sleep I am;
And fearing thus, thus I fall fast asleep.

But at six o'clock, the phone rings in – success!
The Sister tells me our son came up with the sun:
It's a joke she's pleased to make, and so am I.
I see out of the window it's about a quarter high,
And promises another glorious day.

AT THE EDGE OF THE WOOD

First, boys out of school went out of their way home
To detonate the windows; at each smash
Piping with delight and skipping for fright
Of a ghost of the old man popping over his hedge,
Shrieking and nodding from the gate.
Then the game palled, since it was only breaking the silence.
The rain sluiced through the starred gaps,
Crept up walls and into the brick; frost bit and munched;
Weeds craned in and leant on the doors.
Now it is a plot without trees let into the wood
Piled high with tangle and tousle
Buried parapets and roots picking at the last mortar
Though the chimney still stands sheathed in leaves
And you can see for the time being where in a nook
A briony burst its pot with a shower of roots
And back through the press of shrubs and stems
Deep-coils into the woods.

'*Now, we're quite private in here. You can tell me your troubles. The pond, I think you said . . .*'

'We never really liked that pond in the garden. At times it was choked with a sort of weed, which, if you pulled one thread, gleefully unravelled until you had an empty basin before you and the whole of the pond in a soaking heap at your side. Then at other times it was as clear as gin, and lay in the grass staring upwards. If you came anywhere near, the gaze shifted sideways, and it was you that was being stared at, not the empty sky. If you were so bold as to come right up to the edge, swaggering and talking loudly to show you were not afraid, it presented you with so perfect a reflection that you stayed there spellbound and nearly missed dinner getting to know yourself. It had hypnotic powers.'

'*Very well. Then what happened?*'

'Near the pond was a small bell hung on a bracket, which the milkman used to ring as he went out to tell us upstairs in the bedroom that we could go down and make the early-morning tea. This bell was near a little avenue of rose-trees. One morning, very early indeed, it tinged loudly and when I looked out I saw that the empty bottles we had put out the night before were full of bright green pondwater. I had to go down and empty them before the milkman arrived. This was only the beginning. One evening I was astounded to find a brace of starfish coupling on the ornamental stone step of the pool, and, looking up, my cry to my wife to come and look was stifled by the sight of a light peppering of barnacles on the stems of the rose-trees. The vermin had evidently crept there, taking advantage of the thin film of moisture on the ground after the recent very wet weather. I dipped a finger into the pond and tasted it: it was brackish.'

'*But it got worse.*'

'It got worse: one night of howling wind and tempestuous

rain I heard muffled voices outside shouting in rural tones: "Belay there, you lubbers!" "Box the foresail capstan!" "A line! A line! Give me a line there, for Davy Jones' sake!" and a great creaking of timbers. In the morning, there was the garden-seat, which was too big to float, dragged tilting into the pond, half in and half out.'

'But you could put up with all this. How did the change come about?'

'It was getting playful, obviously, and inventive, if ill-informed, and might have got dangerous. I decided to treat it with the consideration and dignity which it would probably later have insisted on, and I invited it in as a lodger, bedding it up in the old bathroom. At first I thought I would have to run canvas troughs up the stairs so it could get to its room without soaking the carpet, and I removed the flap from the letter-box so it would be free to come and go, but it soon learnt to keep its form quite well, and get about in macintosh and goloshes, opening doors with gloved fingers.'

'Until a week ago . . .'

A week ago it started sitting with us in the lounge (and the electric fire had to be turned off, as the windows kept on steaming up). It had accidentally included a goldfish in its body, and when the goggling dolt swam up the neck into the crystal-clear head, it dipped its hand in and fumbled about with many ripples and grimaces, plucked it out, and offered the fish to my wife, with a polite nod. She was just about to go into the kitchen and cook the supper, but I explained quickly that goldfish were bitter to eat, and he put it back. However, I was going to give him a big plate of ice-cubes, which he would have popped into his head and enjoyed sucking, although his real tipple is distilled water, while we watched television, but he didn't seem to want anything. I suppose he thinks he's big enough already.'

'Free board and lodging, eh?'

'I don't know what rent to charge him. I thought I might ask him to join the river for a spell and bring us back some of the money that abounds there: purses lost overboard from pleasure-steamers, rotting away in the mud, and so forth. But he has grown very intolerant of dirt, and might find it difficult to get clean again. Even worse, he might not be able to free himself from his rough dirty cousins, and come roaring back as an impossible green seething giant, tall as the river upended, buckling into the sky, and swamp us and the whole village as well. I shudder to think what would happen if he got as far as the sea, his spiritual home: the country would be in danger. I am at my wits' end, for he is idle, and lounges about all day.'

'Well, that's harmless enough . . .'

'If he's not lounging, he toys with his shape, restlessly. Stripping off his waterproof, he is a charming dolls'-house of glass, with doors and windows opening and shutting; a tree that thrusts up and fills the room; a terrifying shark-shape that darts about between the legs of the furniture, or lurks in the shadows of the room, gleaming in the light of the television-tube; a fountain that blooms without spilling a drop; or, and this image constantly recurs, a very small man with a very large head and streaming eyes, who gazes mournfully up at my wife (she takes no notice), and collapses suddenly into his tears with a sob and a gulp. Domestic, pastoral-phallic, maritime-ghastly, stately-gracious or grotesque-pathetic: he rings the changes on a gamut of moods, showing off, while I have to sit aside slumped in my armchair unable to compete, reflecting what feats he may be able to accomplish in due course with his body, what titillating shapes impose, what exaggerated parts deploy, under his macintosh. I dread the time (for it will come) when I shall arrive home unexpectedly early, and hear a sudden scuffle-away in the waste-pipes, and find my wife ("just out of the shower, dear") with that moist look in her eyes, drying her hair: and then to hear him swaggering in from the garden drains, talking loudly about his day's excursion, as if nothing at all had been going on. For he learns greater charm each day, this Mr Waterman, and can be as stubborn as winter and gentle as the warm rains of spring.'

'I should say that you have a real problem there, but it's too early for a solution yet, until I know you better. Go away, take a week off from the office, spend your time with your wife, relax, eat plenty of nourishing meals, plenty of sex and sleep. Then come and see me again. Good afternoon.

'The next patient, nurse. Ah, Mr Waterman. Sit down, please. Does the gas fire trouble you! No? I can turn it off if you wish. Well now, we're quite private in here. You can tell me your troubles. A married, air-breathing woman, I think you said . . .'

A SILENT MAN

I love the cold; it agrees with me,
I am minded like its petrifaction,
Or do I mean perfection? My heart
Is cold and loves to stroll through cold,
And seems to see a better speech

Rolling in fat clouds of breath.
I keep talk for my walks, silent clouds
That flow in ample, mouthing white
Along the paths. At home
Where I've closeted my wife
And instituted children in the warm
I keep my silence, lest
Those I love, regard, catch cold from me
As though I strolled through mould, and breathing,
Puffed white clouds to spore more fur.
I never take them on my long cold walks alone,
I save them for a warmer time, some kind of spring;
Saved up in me like frozen seeds among
Crisp-flaring turf, stiff marsh, gagged stream,
Paths the skidding ferrule will not prick;
Where floes creak and yearn at floes
To fuse and bind the Thames for walking on.

This narrowing path punctuated with my stick,
This fuming field where in galoshes
I can watch winter tinkle in the stream

And clap its ice across the water-voice
Where it buttocks through the marsh,

And throttle birds, or shoo them south,
Crazing its flat glum sky with trees . . .

And leaves waggled till they snap and drop,
The robin crouching on his back

Fur-legged amid the bristling white,
Horned twig, fence fanged, whetted blades . . .

Fur them of its own even colour
To cling and blur and sheet,

These are my walks;
Where winter acts and silences,

Where all is firming underfoot,
Where I can watch the cold flat water

Fizz into my prints
Till I can shatter crusts; my walks.

THE FORCE

At Mrs Tyson's farmhouse, the electricity is pumped
Off her beck-borne wooden wheel outside.
Greased, steady, it spins within
A white torrent, that stretches up the rocks.
At night its force bounds down
And shakes the lighted rooms, shakes the light;
The mountain's force comes towering down to us.

High near its summit the brink is hitched
To an overflowing squally tarn.
It trembles with stored storms
That pulse across the rim to us, as light.

On a gusty day like this the force
Lashes its tail, the sky abounds
With wind-stuffed rinds of cloud that sprout
Clear force, throbbing in squalls off the sea
Where the sun stands poring down at itself
And makes the air grow tall in spurts
Whose crests turn over in the night-wind, foaming. We spin
Like a loose wheel, and throbbing shakes our light
Into winter, and torrents dangle. Sun
Pulls up the air in fountains, green shoots, forests
Flinching up at it in spray of branches,
Sends down clear water and the loosened torrent
Down into Mrs Tyson's farmhouse backyard,
That pumps white beams off its crest,
In a stiff breeze lashes its tail down the rocks.

THE HOUSE IN THE ACORN

Ah, I thought just as he opened the door
That we all turned, for an instant, and looked away,
Checked ourselves suddenly, then he spoke:
'You're very good to come,' then,
Just for a moment his air thickened,
And he could not breathe, just for the moment.
'My son would have been glad that you came,'
He extended his thick hand, 'Here, all together – '
We are not ourselves or at our ease,
I thought, as we raised our glasses, sipped;
'Help yourselves, please. Please . . .'

'If anyone would care . . .' He stood by the table
Rapping his heavy nails in its polished glare,
'My son is upstairs, at the back of the house,
The nursery, if anyone . . .' I studied
Stocky hair-avenues along my hand-backs,
Wandered through grained plots dappled and sunlit;
'My son . . . sometimes I think they glimpse
Perhaps for a while through sealed lids a few faces
Bending in friendship before it all fades . . .' I nodded,
Slipped out, face averted,

And entered oak aisles; oaken treads
Mounted me up along oaken shafts, lifting me past
Tall silent room upon silent room:
Grained centuries of sunlight toppled to twilight
By chopping and fitting: time turned to timber
And the last oak enclosure with claws of bent oak
Where his white wisp cradled, instantaneous,
Hardly held by his home in its polished housetops.
A breath would have blown him; I held my breath
As I dipped to kiss . . .

Now the instant of this house rolls in my palm
And the company spins in its polished globe
And the drawing-room reels and the house recedes
(Pattering dome-grained out of the oak)
While, ah, as I open the door I hear their close laughter,
Cool earrings swing to the gliding whisper,
More apple-cup chugs from the stouted ewer.

EARTH

By the hearth,
The discomfort of earth, time's fire,
Withers her. She shrinks
Into her eyes, which well and gleam,
Glitter with sleep, sink shut,
Fed by the dry runnels of her face.
The old apple shrivels, but,
For a while, the smell is sweet as blossom,
And the skin soft as warm flowers,
For, as I disturb her sleep, and rise to go,
This goodness wells from the warm eyes
Along the runnels, creating the face:

And as her eyes open and the world returns
So the wrinkles flood over her face
Like earth irrigated with kindliness.

THE CONTENTMENT OF
AN OLD WHITE MAN

The sky is dead. The sky is dead. The sky is dead.
I'm an old white man, if that is your opinion I'm content.
The fat white clouds roll in the old dead sky
They do me good, for all you say they're dead.
They pat my brow. They sweat me a little wet, perchance.
Just as my dazzling beard parades my cheeks, they give me
Ornament. I'm an old white man as well . . .
Dead indeed! You're a sack of wet yourself.
Step on them? Can *you* support the stroll of a razor?
They loll over my brow and childer my thoughts,
Or think I think them, so fond I am – not water-curds,
Thoughts! and correspondence! Dead skins and scurfs
And water-curds . . . but see how fatherly the sunset looks.
They rain, they pass into the ground, you piss,
You pass into the ground, I do, I know my kin,
My great kin, as a microbe is my lesser. Oh,
Lower a little shower and feel some roots, I say,
You've not slept in a bed at my age till you've wet it.
They pass and snort and snow, I'll catch my death
Squatting under a rainshower and pass away
At 105° all rubicund like a sunset. We're all kind,
All water, they're a little quicker, which means
Cleverer, sometimes, don't it? Oh and ah
The graceful fruity woods, cabby! of the clouds,
Snow running on snow and bending as it deepens.
I see I coach among them, my breath sends out;
These woods on mountains, we send up shapes together

Ridge upon ridge, offering them, these clouds,
The only things large enough for God to watch
And judge from, we'd better get there fast. I'm halfway
Being an old white man and here the tree-heads straighten

Slowly and slowly leaf again as
Flickers of white drop off them and
Slowly straighten heads hurting with spring
As their white dreams leave them. Cabby! the clouds rise
Because the sun wants them. Each cloud is unique.

THE HEIR

Now here I am, drinking in the tall old house, alone,
The wide brown river squandering itself outside,
And there's a fine smell of cane chairs and conservatory
dust here,
With the mature thick orchards thriving outside,
And I am drinking, which is a mixture of dreaming and
feeding,
Watching how the stone walls admit all their square glad
answers
To the sun that is alive and thriving outside,
And rests folded in a full pot of beer brimming before me now.
Or it could have been cider, agreed, because of our
thriving orchards,
But it is beer, because of the brewery just down the way
Sipping at the wide brown river all the year round.
So I am a feeder and dreamer both
Of firm thriving apples and of the wide river outside
And of the sun that arrives and rests gladly, folded in my food.

And I agreed to that, and to the passing of the days,
With winged lips of the mist streaming at night, and in
the morning
Thick mists grinding themselves thin, and grinding
themselves to nothing,
For mothers murther us by having us, naturally, and I am glad
to be alive,
Drinking, with the beer squandering itself inside,
Sun folded in upon me and cider thriving among the trees,
And as I am a living man, Mother, I bear you no kind of
a grudge,
Not to you, nor to the good kind cider or beer
Killing me and having me, for you agreed to die, and bear me
no grudge
For being alive and dying, and dying much as you did . . .

38

So I'm glad to sit dreaming and feeding at the wide cane table
                                                              set
For a solid meal that never comes, glad to be spending myself
As the river spends, and the sun pours out, and the ripe fruit
                                                           splits,
Smiling juice sweetly to the hacking wasps, and you did as you
                                                          agreed
Which was to give me life, and I agreed to that too
For the beer agrees with me as I said, and I undertake
To go on agreeing so long as there's passage in my throat.

SWEAT

I sit in the hot room and I sweat,
I see the cool pane bedew with me,
My skin breathes out and pearls the windowpane,
Likes it and clings to it. She comes in,
She loves me and she loves our children too,
And still the sweat is trickling down the pane,
The breath of life makes cooling streaks
And wobbles down the pane. We breathe and burn,
We burn, all together in a hot room,
Our sweat is smoking down the windowpane,
Marks time. I smoke, I stir, and there I write
PR, BR, a streaming heart.
The sun strikes at it down a wide hollow shaft;
Birds swing on the beams, boil off the grass.

ON THE SCREAMING
OF GULLS

The wet wings of birds into the air
Making off from our roofs in the rain
Clapped hard to the drenched flank
In a spray of feather-wet
Must sting the sleek body as they clap.
The muscle-yoke across the back
Stings and spurs the armless animals
And spurs them until they scream
As they do, as they do all night
Whizzing into the mist like chain-shot
That howls where it strikes.
They are ridden upon by their wings,
By their ability for flight,
The wings enjoy the use of them,
Clapped tight around the panting heart.
Brute muscle is the brain, and the brain
In the slippery bright eyes
Mere watcher and recorder
Of muscles on the go, always,
Forcing screams from stung panting sides,
For fish, more fish, fish
Sustaining their spurts across the estuary,
For use, to enjoy the flight
Tight along their screaming mounts.
The gull is delighted in by others,
Ridden by other passengers, parcel of jockey-owners;
The sex jaunts from ground to breeding-ground,

The oval, perfect sex, the thinking egg
Skilled to spin them, bank, and keep their trim
In tight mating flocks
As though furnace were gyroscope,

Compass and owners' orders in one packet;
Compassionate more than the wings,
Mapping no ground, it gives, though the way is lost
Good company in payment.
The weary bird launches its neck
Over the grey rollers.

Cherry-seed, nematode, spore
Of bacilli without number, fern-, alga-spore
Ride too, rafted
To claw, feather, beak
Of this airship
Whose furnace-draught is screams,
Or grow folded into the grey bowel, bilge
And breeder too of the gull's own rotting
Just as it falls, log
Scattered, fluttered
Into unbound leafy bones
Or feathery bones suspended in rut,
Worked to the last instant, thin plans
Surviving pursy passengers.

THE WIDOWER

Yawning, yawning with grief all the time.
The live ones are often alive in fragments
And some of us scream as the weather changes.
Or I raise a frequent steak to my pluming nostrils,
Starving, or yawning, so hungry for air,
Gasping for life. And a snowflake was her friend.
And the sky of clouds hurrying and struggling
Beyond the skylight, were her friends.
She was daytime to the mind,
A light room of trees, spray of water, high flowers
Over a cloudscape, and I brought her
Twelve-hour lyings down for fear of this world,
Head buried in pillows for perfect darkness,
And into this she walked with nothing but advice
And what I called her spells for company.

Ah well, no doubt such happens to many.
Now I myself am alive only in fragments,
A piece of uncertain, of filthy tattered weather.
Pull the clothing to shreds; huddle the tatters together,
Wild and horrible! easily in my rags.

But you said, take another look!
Watch the mixtures, the things moving with one another,
Water running across running water, wind woven on it,
A sudden bleat of black birds marking across the marshes,
Beating wind across water, rooms built of glimmer and
                                    mist there.
I don't say it wouldn't have worked in time,
But my brow knitting it was lighted up my brain,
Mere strain over a surface,
And I just couldn't believe anything, anything at all.
Now look at me!

There's always something there, you said; now let me try
(That leaden waterspout searching so thick and tall
Over the mincing sunny water is no good to anyone)
Some vista of life, some mentality, so let me try now,
Something to watch always, and it's called your spell,
So what do I notice now in my nice quiet room
With the mullions and the college table and the books?
Why, look, there's that exciting queasiness
That queasy vividness of dark windows before thunder:
So I cross over quickly and there I am!
Up among them, the bad clouds over the bright blue,
Adjusting my black pieces over the innocent cricketers
Who tremble like white splinters in the deep gulfs beneath me,
Through the rifting thick platforms. . . . I quite enjoyed that —
But it wasn't true, was it?

All lies, and here the lies come again,
The dead, and the inventions of the dead,
The night, and what the night contains,
The great quivering jelly of resemblances,
The spreading, the too-great majority,
Whose heads hang from memories and nausea,
Who stroll about vomiting, shaking and gaping with it,
Who goggle in terror of their condition, who retire at dawn
To almost inaudible thin quarrels up and down the
                                        graveyard strata
Who lurk with invisible thin whines like gnats in daytime
But who billow through the deep lanes at dusk
Like a mist of bleached portraits, who do not exist,
Who walk like a shivering laundry of shifted humanity
And who stink. . . .

Not true! But thank God the day's come again,
A sunny warm day, a good morning, a morning to recline,
To wear shirts, to look simple and true,
To run hands with definite pleasure

Over the shorn bristly lawn full of mentality,
To plunge conjecture
Easily in a bold search for truth through the lawn's surface,
To consider the small kin, and their place in nature,
The spires and sinews of the worm, how excellent!
Dragging the long cold chain of life for itself,
And the cold speed of its terror,
And the drops of itself massaging into the corridor.
How it spreads under the harrow with no cry!
How it breaks into the bird's beak!
And what sublime sleep, oh marvellous fortitude,
Ever could breed these quiet pallid delving fancies?

And it was joy, one tells me, joy to die,
Moaning and tugging in terror of her condition,
With a thin grip around my ankle out of the turf,
Sinking into the majority, wobbling reminiscences,
And here they come again! because it's the nighttime,
Gelatinous bundles nozzled with portraits
Unconvincing and terrifying, but how many lie there!

You never actually saw one, do you think it's true?
Look for the truth in the lawn, one said, and I don't doubt
                                    she's found it.
Now somebody melts . . . but thinking of death got them
                                    this way
That's what you're saying, in these environs,
These parts of the mind, any mind, these fancies,
Thinking of horrors created them horrors.

Love frightens them, so let's frighten them.
It frightens them because it's so mysterious.
It frightens me. You are a shapely white.
Oh, I droop with admiration. No, no, I spring!
That kills them . . . and are you really there?
Yes, especially there. What happens then?

It makes them so thin. They are gone from themselves.
Did I frighten you then? Everyone fears.
Two is a round reality. Dead is a nonsense.
But a real one. And one of us is dead.

DECREATOR

Grown-up idiot, see the slow-motion of him,
And that slow-motion sludge of a tongue
Coiling along its stream of happenings,
Head lolling and tongue lolling,
Sudden brightenings, lurches. He was brisk,
Carried his headpiece like a haughty dish,
Suddenly his brain churned thick
And with a dull chime his brain turned over
A clucking and he sat down suddenly.
His poll curdled with a dull clack,
Cocked listening, a crooked cork of the neck,
A lid flipped. Not a spatter of larks
Rising, cheerily callous and irresponsible, nor melodramatic
Red entrails labouring, living brain split
All over, like a hairnet, bolting out of the ears –
Though the red mouth chewed, clack,
And the raw eyes soaked suddenly –
But a dull cluck and a dull kind of clay twisted
And skeined into a surprise and twirled up to
And round and round a wide stare.

Thereafter he was to wander
With a hesitation at either elbow
And a little free-wheeling spittle
Through a kind of pastoral, in the parks of patrons,
By their dusty greenhouses, bubbling glassy streams,
Springing up in odd corners, by snivelly taps,

Serious avenues. Their doves
Would babble off their lawns at him, their crones
Croon to him over the spinning,
Their tapping blind pensioners fall nodding as he came
                                        up to them

Leaky-lipped, faulty, and no part of it at all.
For one ordinary Sunday strolling
He looked down himself as with a dull crash
His brain fell several floors and stopped
And he sat down suddenly. It was a glance
From the sinewy confident husband and the rolling pram
Hooded like a whelk and pearly, started it, its scrap
Of white meat and fluff lodged in recesses and the woman
Fluffed on the man's arm
Like a floss of him, and he an elbow of her,
And the face-bone with its marrow of eyes,
Stare-marrow, and the lurking look in the whelk,
The same look, and all six with the one stare,
One flesh with six eyes, one person
In three stares, and the creation all rolled of it,
And he looked down himself and the creation trundled
Uphill at him and he looked
Down at himself and he sat down
Suddenly and his brain dropped several storeys
Burst the front door and pitched away downhill.

THE CASE

for Roy Hart

'Man . . . is an experiment and a transition. He is nothing else than the
narrow and perilous bridge between nature and spirit. His innermost
destiny drives him on to the spirit and to God. His innermost longing
draws him back to nature, the mother. Between the two forces his life
hangs tremulous and irresolute.'

(Hermann Hesse, *Steppenwolf*)

I am a gardener,
A maker of trials, flowers, hypotheses.
I water the earth.
I raise perfumes there.
Mother told me to stand, and I did so,
Stepping towards the window in which she sat.
'Now, did you find him, your other half?
And mine,' she said, and I shook my head:
'No, my time is so short and I'll take no oath.'
'You've just taken one, by standing,
My dear one,' she said, and she told me how the stars
Had said as much, and I concurred and saw
How the crystalware of the polished table,
The cabinets of glass things walling the room,
The tall roses beyond the glass, the gloss of the table,
Had said as much in sunshine from my first tottering.
So she lifted my hand and kissed it and said I was to be celibate,
And this was great good fortune and I was a good child
For I had a quest and few had as much.
The roses nodded.

So I became a gardener,
A maker of prayers, flowers, hypotheses.
A gardener 'washed in my fertile sweat',
My hair of an opulent brown 'like the Lord's,

That makes you think of fertile fields.'
And among the flowers, in the walled garden, 'This is life!' she
cried,
'What a shame, oh what a shame,' she said,
'What a shame we have to die,' she cried, all
The flowers pumping and pumping their natures into her,
Into her nostrils, winged wide, she leaning,
Leaning back, breathing deeply, blushing deeply,
Face shining and deep breath and tall brick
Holding the air still and the heat high in a tall room.

And I swam in the thunderstorm in the river of blood, oil and
cider,
And I saw the blue of my recovery open around me in the water
Blood, cider, rainbow, and the apples still warm after sunset
Dashed in the cold downpour, and so this mother-world
Opened around me and I lay in the perfumes after rain out of
the river
Tugging the wet grass, eyes squeezed, straining to the glory,
The burst of white glory like the whitest clouds rising to the sun

And it was like a door opening in the sky, it was like a door
opening in the water,
It was like the high mansion of the sky, and water poured from
the tall french windows.
It was like a sudden smell of fur among the flowers, it was like a
face at dusk
It was like a rough trouser on a smooth leg. Oh, shame,
It was the mother-world wet with perfume. It was something
about God.

And she stood there and I wanted to tell her something
and she was gone
It was something about God. She stood smiling on the wet verge
And she waited for me to tell her but she was gone.
And three gusts of hot dry air came almost without sound

Through the bushes, and she went. Through the bushes
Of blown and bruised roses. And she went. And the bushes
were blown
And the gusts were hot, dry air, nearly black with perfume,
Alive with perfume. Oh shame. It was like an announcement,
Like an invitation, an introduction, an invitation, a quick smile
in the dusk.
It was like a door opening on a door of flowers that opened on
flowers that were opening.
It was like the twist of a rosy fish among lily-pads that were
twisting on their deep stems.
The rosy goldfish were there in the dusky pond, but she was
gone.
It was something about God. My hand made a wet door in the
water
And I thought of something I knew about God. My mother
Stared at me from the pool over my shoulder and when I
turned she was gone.
Then the wind blew three hot dry gusts to me through the
broken rose-bushes
And she came to me dusky with perfume and I walked toward
her
And through her, groping for her hand. And it was something
about God.
And I searched in my head for it with my eyes closed. But it
was gone.

And I became a gardener, a hypothesiser, one who would
consult his sensations,
For 'we live in sensations and where there are none there is no
life,'
One with the birds that are blue-egged because they love
the sky!
With the flocks of giraffes craning towards the heavens!
With the peacocks dressed in their love for the high sun
And in their spectra of the drifting rains, one

With the great oaks in my keeping that stretched up to touch
God!

And one who could look up gladly and meet God's gaze,
His wide blue gaze, through my blood, as I think;
And God was silent and invisible and I loved him for it,
I loved him for his silent invisibility, for his virile restraint,
And I was one with my peacocks that sent out their wild cry
Sounding like shrill 'help!' and meaning no such thing,
While my flocks of deer wrote love in their free legs
Their high springy haunches and bounding turf. And they
would pause
And look upwards, and breathe through wide nostrils, and all
day
It was wide and firm and in God's gaze and open: tussock and
turf, long lake,
Reed-sigh, silence and space, pathway and flower furnace
Banked up and breathing.

And the people. And the causeway into the walled garden.
And the people walking in so slowly, on their toes
Through the wide doorway, into the cube of still air,
Into the perspective of flowers, following each other in
groups,
Gazing around, 'Oh, what shame, to die!' and the great doorway
And ourselves, smiling, and standing back, and they changed,
Concentrated, concentrating, at the edges of the body, the rims
Tighter, clearer, by the sensations of their bodies, solidified,
bound,
Like the angels, the bodies' knowledge of the flowers inbound
Into its tightening and warming at the heart of flowers, the fire
called

'Then-shall-ye-see-and-your-heart-shall-rejoice-
And-your-bones-shall-sprout-as-the-blade . . .'

And she was gone. And she lay down like the earth after rain.
It was love-talk in every grain. And something about God.

The brick walls creaked in the wind, grain to grain.
And judgment came as the father comes, and she is gone.
Clouds swoop under the turf into the pond, the peacock cries
'Help!' strutting in its aurora, love talks
Grain to grain, gossiping about judgment, his coming. Ranges
Tumble to boulders that rattle to shingles that ease to wide
                                                            beaches
That flurry to dust that puffs to new dusts that dust
To dusting dust, all talking, all
Gossiping of glory, and there are people
In the gardens, in white shirts, drifting,
Gossiping of shame through the gardens, 'Oh glory!'

Through the gardens . . . Well, father, is that how you come?
Come then.
Whose breath is it that flares through the shrubberies?
Whose breath that returns? Look at the people
All ageing to judgment, all
Agreeing to judgment. Look at that woman
Still snuffing up the flowers. My mother!
Look at her. She bends backwards to the tall flowers, falls.
Her flower-laden breath returns to the skies.
I think this garden is a prayer,
Shall I burn it as an offering?
And I think these people are a prayer,
I think they are a message.
Shall I burn them for their syllable?
There is a fire crying 'shame!' here already!
It mixes dying with flowering.
I think we husk our uttering. I think
We tip it out. Our perfect syllable,
Tripped out over the death-bed, a one,
Round, perfectly-falling silence.
Look how they seek the glory over these flowers!
I wanted to say something about God,
My syllable about God. I think

We are a prayer. I think
He wants his breath back, unhusked
Of all the people, our dying silences,
Our great involuntary promise
Unhusked, flying out into the rain, over the battlefields,
Switching through shrubberies, into the sky . . .

You press, oh God!
You press on me as I press on an eyeball,
You press sunsets and autumns and dying flowers,
You press lank ageing people in gardens 'Oh shame
To die,' you feather roses and matchflames like wisps of your
                                                fingers,
Your great sun cuffs age at us. I will bring,
I will bring you in, father, through the bounds of my senses,
Face to face, father, through the sockets of my head,
Haul you in, father, through my eyes with my fingers,
Into my head through my eyes, father, my eyes, oh my eyes . . .

To live in the blind sockets, the glorious blunt passages,
Tended by gardeners, nostril, eye, mouth,
Bruised face in a white shirt ageing,
To be called 'Father' and to hear call high
'Oh shame, what a shame, to die' as they see the great flowers,
To hear the peacock 'help!' that means no such thing,
And to live unseeing, not watching, without judging, called
                                                'Father'.

CHRISTIANA

for Barbara

That day in the Interpreter's house, in one of his Significant
Rooms,
There was naught but an ugly spider hanging by her hands on
the wall,
And it was a spacious room, the best in all the house.
'Is there but one spider in all this spacious room?'
And then the water stood in my eyes
And I thought how like an ugly creature I looked
In what fine room soever I was,
And my heart crept like a spider.

And my heart crept like a spider into the centre of my web
And I sat bell-tongued there and my sound
Was the silvery look of my rounds and radii,
And I bent and sucked some blood, but I did it
With care and elegance like a crane unloading vessels;
I set myself on damask linen and I was lost to sight there,
And I hugged my legs astride it, wrapping the pearl-bunch
round;
I skated on the water with legs of glass, and with candystriped
legs
Ran through the dew like green racks of glass cannonball;
And I saw myself hanging with trustful hands
In any room in every house, hanging on by faith
Like wolfhounds that were dwarfs, or stout shaggy oats,
And I wept to have found so much of myself ugly
In the trustful beasts that are jewel-eyed and full of clean
machinery,
And thought that many a spacious heart was ugly
And empty without its tip-toe surprise of spiders
Running like cracks in the universe of a smooth white ceiling,
And how a seamless heart is like a stone.

And the Interpreter saw
The stillness of the water standing in her eyes,
And said,
Now you must work on Beelzebub's black flies for Me.

MINERALS OF CORNWALL,
STONES OF CORNWALL

A case of samples

Splinters of information, stones of information,
Drab stones in a drab box, specimens of a distant place,
Granite, galena, talc, lava, kaolin, quartz,
Landscape in a box, under the dull sky of Leeds –
One morning was awake, in Cornwall, by the estuary,
In the tangy pearl-light, tangy tin-light,
And the stones were awake, these ounce-chips,
Had begun to think, in the place they came out of.

Tissues of the earth, in their proper place,
Quartz tinged with the rose, the deep quick,
Scrap of tissue of the slow heart of the earth,
Throbbing the light I look at it with,
Pumps slowly, most slowly, the deep organ of the earth;
And galena too, snow-silvery, its chipped sample
Shines like sun on peaks, it plays and thinks with the
mineral light,
It sends back its good conclusions, it is exposed,
It sends back the light silked and silvered,
And talc, and kaolin, why they are purged, laundered,
As I see the white sand of some seamless beaches here
Is laundered and purged like the whole world's mud
Quite cleansed to its very crystal; talc a white matt,
Kaolin, the white wife of Cornwall
Glistening with inclusions, clearly its conclusions
Considered and laid down, the stone-look
Of its thoughts and opinions of flowers
And turf riding and seeding above it in the wind,
Thoughts gathered for millennia as they blossomed in millions
Above its then kaolin-station within the moor,
The place of foaming white streams and smoking blanched
mountains.

Asbestos had found this bright morning
Its linear plan of fibres, its simple style,
Lay there, declaring, like the others;
Granite, the great rock, the rock of rocks,
At home now, flecked green, heavily contented in its box,
Riding with me high above its general body,
The great massif, while its fellows, the hills of it
Rise high around us; nor was lava silent
Now it remembered by glistening in this light
Boiling, and was swart with great content

Having seen God walking over the burning marl, having seen
A Someone thrusting his finger into the mountainside
To make it boil – here is the issue of this divine intrusion,
I am the issue of this divine intrusion,
My heart beats deep and fast, my teeth
Glisten over the swiftness of my breath,
My thoughts hurry like lightning, my voice
Is a squeak buried among the rending of mountains,
I am a mist passing through the crevices of these great seniors
Enclosed by me in a box, now free of the light, conversing
Of all the issue this homecoming has awakened in the stone mind
The mines like frozen bolts of black lightning deep in the land
Saying, and the edge of their imaginings cuts across my mind:
We are where we were taken from, and so we show ourselves
Ringing with changes and calls of fellowship
That call to us ton to ounce across Cornish valleys.

The valleys throng with the ghosts of stone so I may scarcely
pass,
Their loving might crush, they cry out at their clumsiness,
Move away, death-dealing hardnesses, in love.
The house is full of a sound of running water,
The night is a black honey, crystals wink at the brim,
A wind blows through the clock, the black mud outside
Lies curled up in haunches like a sleeping cat.

SHADOW-SILK

Rapid brothy whispers in the bed.
It was like silk splitting in me.
The house is full of the sound of running water.
A wind blows through the clock.
It is like a frail leaf-skeleton
Shivering in a casket.
We are heels over ears in love.
The window-frame blackens.
Below, the trees flood darkly,
The wind butts in the curtain
A doddering forehead.
We have a one candle.
Your hair is like a weir,
Or fields of posture,
In terrace upon terrace
Rising forest murmur,
And across the garden
Frothily flows the ghost.
The night is black honey,
Presses hard on the glass.
A sudden set! The stars are out.
This is too much; adventuring nectars
Wink with packed crystals
That hang depth upon depth
Age clotting the frame.
I must close this picture-book.
I must wade through these shadows.
Black springs from the corners
Brim the quartz-crystals
Engorge the ewers
Flood from the cupboards
Soaking the dresses
Pile under the bed

In black satin cushions.
That candle is unsnuffable!
We are afloat!
But the ring on your finger
Spins without stirring,
I pad through the undertow
Reach out and close
That heavenly almanac.
Our wonder still lingers
Over the covers
As within the pages
All the stars glitter.
A wind blows through the clock
And across the garden
Frothily flows the ghost.

THE MOON DISPOSES

(Perranporth beach)

The mountainous sand-dunes with their gulls
Are all the same wind's moveables,
The wind's legs climb, recline,
Sit up gigantic, we wade
Such slithering pockets our legs are half the size,
There is an entrance pinched, a plain laid out,
An overshadowing of pleated forts.
We cannot see the sea, the sea-wind stings with sand,
We cannot see the moon that swims the wind,
The setting wave that started on the wind, pulls back.

Another slithering rim, we tumble whirling
A flying step to bed, better than harmless,
Here is someone's hoofprint on her hills
A broken ring with sheltering sides
She printed in the sand. A broken ring. We peer from play.

Hours late we walk among the strewn dead
Of this tide's sacrifice. There are strangled mussels:
The moon pulls back the lid, the wind unhinges them,
They choke on fans, they are bunched blue, black band.
The dead are beautiful, and give us life.
The setting wave recoils
In flocculence of blood-in-crystal,
It is medusa parched to hoofprints, broken bands,
Which are beautiful, and give us life.
The moon has stranded and the moon's air strangled
And the beauty of her dead dunes sent us up there
Which gave us life. Out at sea
Waves flee up the face of a far sea-rock, it is a pure white door
Flashing in the cliff-face opposite,
Great door, opening, closing, rumbling open, moonlike
Flying open on its close.

YOUNG WOMEN WITH THE
HAIR OF WITCHES AND
NO MODESTY

'I loved Ophelia!'

I have always loved water, and praised it.
I have often wished water would hold still.
Changes and glints bemuse a man terribly:
There is champagne and glimmer of mists;
Torrents, the distaffs of themselves, exalted, confused;
And snow splintering silently, skilfully, indifferently.
I have often wished water would hold still.
Now it does so, or ripples so, skilfully
In cross and doublecross, surcross and countercross.
A person lives in the darkness of it, watching gravely;

I used to see her straight and cool, considering the pond,
And as I approached she would turn gracefully
In her hair, its waves betraying her origin.
I told her that her thoughts issued in hair like consideration of
                                                                    water,
And if she laughed, that they would rain like spasms of
                                                                    weeping,
Or if she wept, then solemnly they held still,
And in the rain, the perfumes of it, and the blowing of it,
Confused, like hosts of people all shouting.
In such a world the bride walks through dressed as a
                                                                    waterfall,
And ripe grapes fall and splash smooth snow with jagged
                                                                    purple,
Young girls grow brown as acorns in their rainy climb
                                                        towards oakhood,
And brown moths settle low down among ivories wet with
                                                                    love.

But she loosened her hair in a sudden tangle of contradictions,
In cross and doublecross, surcross and countercross,
And I was a shadow in the twilight of her late displeasure.
I asked water to stand still, now nothing else holds.

THE YOUTHFUL SCIENTIST
REMEMBERS

After a day's clay my shoes drag like a snail's skirt
And hurt as much on gravel. You have mud on your
                                            jersey,
This pleases me, I cannot say why. Summer-yolk
Hangs heavy in the sky, ready to rupture in slow swirls,
Immense custard: like the curious wobbly heart
Struggling inside my pink shirt. Spring is pink,
                                            predominately,
And frothy, thriving, the glorious forgotten sound of healing,
And cheering, all shouting and cheering. With what
                                            inwardness
The shadows of autumn open, brown and mobile as cognac,
And the whole of my beer comes reeling up to me in one great
                                            amber rafter
Like a beam of the purest sun, well-aged; as it travels the
                                            grass
The dead smile an immense toothy underground, kindly.
I cannot explain why. You pointed out that the lily
Was somebody's red tail inside their white nightie
                    So much so
That I am still sober and amazed at the starlight glittering in
                                            the mud,
I am amazed at the stars, and the greatest wonder of them all
Is that their black is as full as their white, the black
Impends with the white, packing between the white,
And under the hives of silence there are swarms of light,
And padded between black comb, struggling white.

I cannot explain this, with the black as full as the bright,
The mud as full as the sunlight. I had envisaged
Some library of chemistry and music
With lean lithe scores padding the long pine shelves,

Plumage of crystal vials clothing strong deal tables;
Had thought that the stars would only tug at me slightly,
Or sprinkle thin clear visions about me for study –
Instead you point at that flower, your dress fits like a clove.

THE IDEA OF ENTROPY AT
MAENPORTH BEACH

'C'est Elle! noire et pourtant lumineuse.'
to John Layard

A boggy wood as full of springs as trees.
Slowly she slipped into the muck.
It was a white dress, she said, and that was not right.
Leathery polished mud, that stank as it split.
It is a smooth white body, she said, and that is not right,
Not quite right; I'll have a smoother,
Slicker body, and my golden hair
Will sprinkle rich goodness everywhere.
So slowly she backed into the mud.

If it were a white dress, she said, with some little black,
Dressed with a little flaw, a smut, some swart
Twinge of ancestry, or if it were all black
Since I am white, but – it's my mistake.
So slowly she slunk, all pleated, into the muck.

The mud spatters with rich seed and ranging pollens.
Black darts up the pleats, black pleats
Lance along the white ones, and she stops
Swaying, cut in half. Is it right, she sobs
As the fat, juicy, incredibly tart muck rises
Round her throat and dims the diamond there?
It is right, so she stretches her white neck back
And takes a deep breath once and a one step back.
Some golden strands afloat pull after her.

The mud recoils, lies heavy, queasy, swart.
But then this soft blubber stirs, and quickly she comes up
Dressed like a mound of lickerish earth,
Swiftly ascending in a streaming pat

That grows tall, smooths brimming hips, and steps out
On flowing pillars, darkly draped.
And then the blackness breaks open with blue eyes
Of this black Venus rising helmeted in night
Who as she glides grins brilliantly, and drops
Swatches superb as molasses on her path.

Who is that negress running on the beach
Laughing excitedly with teeth as white
As the white waves kneeling, dazzled, to the sands?
Clapping excitedly the black rooks rise,
Running delightedly in slapping rags
She sprinkles substance, and the small life flies!

She laughs aloud, and bares her teeth again, and cries:
Now that I am all black, and running in my richness
And knowing it a little, I have learnt
It is quite wrong to be all white always;
And knowing it a little, I shall take great care
To keep a little black about me somewhere.
A snotty nostril, a mourning nail will do.
Mud is a good dress, but not the best.
Ah, watch, she runs into the sea. She walks
In streaky white on dazzling sands that stretch
Like the whole world's pursy mud quite purged.
The black rooks coo like doves, new suns beam
From every droplet of the shattering waves,
From every crystal of the shattered rock.
Drenched in the mud, pure white rejoiced,
From this collision were new colours born,
And in their slithering passage to the sea
The shrugged-up riches of deep darkness sang.

THE HOUSE OF TAPS

to P.D.S.

In the house of the Reverend Earth and Dr Waters
Moonlight strikes from the taps.
In the daytime, it is sunlight, full clear beams of it!
When they give water, these faucets, it is holy water,
Or river water, with green shadows of great ship-hulls gliding
in it.
There are some also that bundle out exceptional ripe golden
cornsheaves
And blackberries also, and pineapples and nightshade and
innumerable other kinds of berries.
There is a large curved one like morning glory full of strong
birdsong
And the smell of woodsmoke mixed with wet nettles.
Others I would not turn on again, not if you paid me, there
are some
That throw out glittering lead, or rushes of fire,
And these are all made of wood, so that they smoke and scorch
as they run,
And if they char too far they can never be turned off again.
There is another which is the faucet of pouring darkness, my
eyes dim,
I grope, can I ever find it again to stop the darkness coming?
And there is yet another and this is the worst that seems to give
out nothing
But when you look round there are certain articles missing.
But mostly they give out good things, sunshine and earth,
Or milk, or fine silky stuffs that glide out rustling,
The sleeping evening sounds of a town on the edge of the
country
With rooks cawing as they settle, the clank of a pail, a snatch
of radio music,

(Though I remember another that turned on a soft and
                                    continuous cursing
And from it extruded a pallid foul-mouthed person
Whose mouth foamed as I turned him off at the chest . . .)

But so many of them turn out good things, there is no majority
Of flowing blood or raw gobbets of flesh, it is mostly
Womansong, a stream of laughter or of salmon or bright blue
                                    pebbles –
And the lion-headed spigot that gushes mead and mead-hall
                                    laughter –
There are so many giving moonlight and in the day bright
                sunlight, rich dark barley-wine, and dew . . .
Is this house of personages that prefer tenants to use the taps
                                    and sample the waters
And best of all to install faucets running with their own
                                    personal tastes and choices,
In the great house of the Reverend Mrs Earth and Doctor Waters

THE WIZARD'S NEW MEETING

I am startled by comparisons.
Ice melts from the thatches with the bare restraint
With which the flesh disquantities.
The sound of it beats back like small hearts in sheer spaces.
Stars lie in pools black as pupils
That return their stare, ice-irised. Though nearby
Fire thaws out the greenwood, slow explosion
Of smoke lifts through the chimney, here
My slow trudge snaps snow-crust and prints white darkly;
Blanched breath trudges across the night sky.
Things shiver and my breath is negatived;
In spread hand I hold the pane.

I slam the door. The brazier sucks
And glows in storeys.
I have the hair, the wax, a specimen of writing,
A pane of ice from the flooded churchyard.
I cast them in, they begin to wreck
And flicker with thin films, a gold stain spreads.
What do I think will happen, but steam and smoke?
I utter the words of vertigo, were I so strong
I should vomit as I spoke them, as some are said to,
Vomit as a thorough utterance. I am unsuitable,
But I will lend it blood.

The great book opens of its own accord,
Its snow-light floods the room, it comes, it comes,
The past has ripped away, there is a thin snow curling
And recurling over jagged mines
Of reserved lightning, I see boiling eyes
And a puckered mouth shouting silence so I razor,
The bowl fills and I grow colder

And the squalling bends to sip. I will not speak in terror
For looks of terror terrify the dead
To look so terrible, so I've studied calm,
Studied quietness till the right time comes
Which gives me calm. I am magic, then:

Magic enough to greet a person from the scraps and bones
Someone risen out of the feast of coals, a person
Fallen through our festering death, but risen up
And singing gladly of her current death.

TELL ME, DOCTOR

'Dew on dead bodies: big joy' (Zolar's Dream Book)
DOCTOR SOLUS

What do you make of the petals on the body, doctor?
She grew in the mirror at my back.
The dead body wet with dew made a humped shape
A wide-eyed body strewed with wet petals at the tree's foot
Like severed eyelids, so many eyelids
Shucked off and still we couldn't see. She grew
Old in the mirror, now I watch it empty over my back
And see only blank volumes, wide doors and staring ceilings
An unhealing blank place in the mirror,
And no she at my back. I was surprised at first
To feel my tears, until they grew like roots
Feeding to my mouth for nourishment, the salt taste
And the throbbing breakdown: I was surprised at first
To find my groin stir at the dead wet body
As if it wanted and began to seek out new life.
What do you make of the petals on the body,
Doctor? What of the dew wetting this dead body?
Should we not try to open our eyes under these showering
Dead things, doctor, as we shuck the old body off its back,
This blank place on the ground, as now we brush the petals
                                             off the face? Brush
The so many eyelids from the sightless face, doctor,
Brush scales off one pair of eyes at least.

THE FLIGHT OF WHITE
SHADOWS

Over the crooked notice-board crying 'Private',
Over 'Greenlease' one half rented to the weeds
That munch its shivering windows, over the wide flat
                                                waters
Streaked by the gulls with long white cries,
Tripling the reed-hiss, killing the reflections,
The brusque shower comes. Each drop binds in itself
A terrestrial globe for nobody's inspection
Incurving sky full of meadow, gravid horse, farm, folk
                                                focused, each
Splashes itself many times over in leaves,
On rocks, worlds out of worlds, into worlds, before entering
The troubled horsetrough or the lying-down ditch
Still and long, that held a slightly vaster
Version of the sky. It is not a day for reflections,
Not even the smallest, of bird-bath, hoofprint, flowercup,
So slaughtered by swarming lives, the little bombs
Hacking away, whose twinkling self-assassinations
Tumble like consequences; confluences
Threading through tree-towers. A flap of thunder
Shakes out the clouds in the greatest of them all
Who, when in smooth vein, binds the sky into one salt,
One ferociously-curving whole whose theme is high sun
Boring his windy fire-holes – today is roof and ceiling,
Tiled and shattered snowing,
Racing acute edges on to the seashore.

Hordes strike, and forget themselves immediately, are gone
Water into water, or into stone speckling without sympathy,
So what afterlife for the vehemence of sheer-fall,
The blackener of the sky with the limpid on earth,
Spater, bridge-bungler, gouger of fellow-water,

Bruised eggs streaming with a thin vision,
Smashed fruit under black banners? The same, though
Drawn through rock, honeycombs of knives,
Staircases of razors, chasms of scimitars,
Sandy scythe-galleries, division and redivision,
Unlikely rejoinings, green amnesias – all
To the one reflection down river-paths,
Passed down by the rivers, down to that larger,
To the vastation, which is not
The same artist for an instant either.

THE HAUNTED ARMCHAIR

'. . . and hid his lord's money . . .' (Matthew 25)

I want it not it not to go wrong. I want nothing to go wrong.
I shall guard and hedge and clip to the end of my days
So that nothing goes wrong. This body, this perfect body
That came from my mother's womb undiseased, wholesome,
No, nothing must go wrong. It is not I. It is not I.
No, it is not I. I is lodged in its head's centre,
Its turret, a little towards its eyes; it is not I, it is not I but it is
                                                              mine
And an over-ranking shame to disease it, to let it disease.
I wash my hands, I wash my hands, I wash my hands once,
                                                     twice, thrice,
I rinse my eyes with the sterile saline; I close, I pull the thick
                                                              curtain,
I close the door and lock it, once, twice, thrice, I sit, I lie, I sleep
in the great armchair,
And I sleep. Sleep, sleep is the preservative, cultivate sleep, it
keeps me perfect.
No, no, it is not I; I lives only in the turret;
It is the body, it is the body, it is the body is the loved thing,
It is from my mother, it is my mother's
It came from my mother, it is an organ of the body of my
                                                              mother
And I shall keep it with no rough touch upon it
No rough disease to ramp up and down in it. The world?
And the world? That is the mind's. In the turret. And now I
                                                         will sleep.
I will sleep now, for my body exists. That is enough.
Something wakes me. Is it the fire?
It crackles like a speech. The buffet of winds, the cracks
Of the beams, the taste of the sun, the swimming shark of the
                                                              moon?

No, I think, no, I think, I think I hear time flowing,
No, I think I hear time eroding, the cinder withering in the
grate,
The grate withering with the time, my hands raised to my eyes
Where my eyes are withering, I look close at my withering
hands. How long?
How much time have I seen withering? Did I come here today?
Suddenly everything grants me withering. Shall I sit here
again?
The body is gone. I sit here alone. A nothing, a virgin
memory.
A grease-spot. A dirty chair-back.

FRANKENSTEIN IN THE FOREST

'I am afraid for the meat
Of my illegitimate son
In the warm autumn.
When will the lightning come?'
Much wisdom had congregated there
In the open-air laboratory which is a cemetery
Under the great oaks
In the litter of acorns:
Mute parcels of impending forests.
There are grim-mouthed toads
Flocked round a boulder of quartz
Deep, complex and prodigious
That gloams in its depths
And twitches there as with a flutter of lightning.
On a portable radio
The size of a hymn-book
A harpsichord plays Scarlatti,
It suffers an attack of amnesia
As the lightning steers near.
The darkness has eaten everything except his face
The alert wise face
Backed by a view of tossing trees,
The bones of his skull
Are as loose as the leaves of the forest,
'I will send lightning through him
It will live under his skin
It will heal his mouldering
Undead bric-à-brac of other men.

There are so many bibles
Without a crack of light;
Mine has pages of slate
With fossils clearly inscribed,
Leather from racehorses
And crocodiles,
Thin frying leaves of electricity
That lies obediently in its place
Man-skin, oak-bark and quartz. . .'
The marble grave-stones
Are covered with equations
In the master's quick black analytick crayon,
Their stone books open at only one page;
'It is my great lightning son
Dressed in metal and bark
And the limbs of departed men,
Lightning peers out of his eyes;
He will heal their mouldering.
It is time
To raise him on the sizzling platform.'
The lightning makes a blue cave of the forest,
It strikes violently at a hawthorn tree,
A sweet smell fills the air,
It has blossomed heavily.
Now the bright blue
Thistling sparks have stuck to his poles,
His crystal machine
Fills with spangled golden oil.
His golden beehives' buzz rises to a wail
And the monster ascends on its winches,
The clouds draw up their heavy black pews
The rain falls
And the lightning services.

The storm clears.

Cloud-men are digging
Deep blue graves in the sky.
Out of the machine steps
The man, mute, complex and prodigious,
His clothes flickering with electricity,
His first murder not due until tomorrow.

Humming water holds the high stars.
Meteors fall through the great fat icicles.
Spiders at rest from skinny leg-work
Lean heads forward on shaggy head-laces
All glittering from an askew moon in the sky:
One hinge snapped; a white door dislocated.
The night leans forward on this thin window;
Next door, tattered glass,
Wind twittering on jagged edges.
Doors beat like wings wishing to rise.
I lean forward to this thin fire.
A woman leaves – even the flames grow cool –
She is a one hinge snapped, I am a half-scissors.

SIX ODES

I TABLE-LADY

I sent her into the wine-glass to listen.
I prodded her into the apple-burrow; I told her to take out her
      pin-dagger as soon as she heard the maggot chewing.
I gave her a bath in a walnut-shell.
She made a salt-necklace, piercing the crystals together.
I was frightened when she fell into the mustard, but I rolled
      her clean on a piece of bread.
I told her to sit in the cruet like an information kiosk and
      answer some questions.
I compiled a savoury blanc-mange for her studded with
      angelica; it was a gobbet of my fish-sauce.
But she ran from the reek of my steak, the evisceration of an
      elephant; I gave her a cress-leaf fan.
She got drunk in a grape. I found her snoring like a scarlet fly
      on her back in the skin like a flabby canoe.
It was after I had eaten the blood-orange that I missed her.

II WATER-LADY

He asked her to go into the wood and tell him what she saw
      there.
She walked between the trees and the first thing she liked was
      the pond.
She knelt down and stripped off the thin film of reflections,
      rolled it up and put it into her pocket to show she
      had been there.
The water's new skin reflected with more brilliance and better
      colour.
So she knelt down and took this new skin and put it into her
      pocket, throwing the other skin away.
But the colours of the newest skin were without equal so she
      took this instead.

In due time she emptied the pond in this manner.

All that was left was a slippery hole, a sloppy quag with a few
fish skipping.

She felt sorry for the fish so she went down into the quag and
captured them in her skirt and climbed out.

Then she looked for where the torn scraps of reflection had
settled among the undergrowth and she slid a fish
into each one.

After she had done this she went back to him. 'What are those
stains on your skirt?' were his first words . . .

But his suspicious were drowned in amazement as she unrolled
the tapestry of reflections for him.

III HOWDAH-LADY

A little bloodstained clockwork in a puddle of blood.

She picked it up sighing, wiped it on her skirt.

Look, she said, it's all that's left of Peter, I wonder what could
have done it?

I shrugged my heavy shoulders.

I don't know, she said, whether one can give a piece of
machinery a proper burial. Might it not be better,
she sniggered, to fasten it in a memorial clock,
so that one always thought of poor Peter as one
looked at the time?

My eye itched, I rubbed it with my ear.

I suppose he was thrown from his elephant, she said, placing
one tiny foot in the crook of my trunk, and when they
dragged him away this piece remained.

I hoisted her to my back.

But I don't want the beastly thing, she cried from the howdah,
and she flung the clockwork into the swamp.

As we left, I saw it turn into a golden beetle that buzzed off into
a belt of wild nasturtiums.

She wears the long series of wonder-awakening dresses,
She wears the fishskin cloak,
She wears the gown of pearl with the constellations slashed
                                   into its dark lining,
She undresses out of the night sky, each night of the year a
                                   different sky,
She wears altitude dresses and vertigo dresses,
She plucks open the long staircase at the neck with the big
     buttons of bird-skulls in the white dress of sow-thistle.
She has leather britches known to be chimp-skin,
She has combed star-rays into a shaggy night-dress,
She has a bodice of bone-flounces, a turbinal blouse through
                                   which the air pours.
There is a gown she has that shimmers without slit or seam like
                                   the wall of an aquarium:
A starfish moves slowly on its pumps across her bosom,
A shark glides, a turtle rows silently between her knees,
And she adopts in turn the long dress of sewn louse-skin,
The romper suit of purple jam packed with tiny oval seeds,
The foggy grey dress, and lapping between its folds
Echo bird-cries and meteor-noises and declarations of love,
The ballgown of ticker-tape,
The evening dress of flexible swirling clockwork running
                                   against time,
The cocktail dress of bloody smoke and bullet-torn bandages,
And the little black dress of grave-soil that rends and seals
                                   as she turns.
Often she sits up all night in the philosopher's library
Sewing strong patches from his wardrobes of thought
Into her wounded dresses.

V LEARNING-LADY

I sprained my wrist taking her skirt off; it was moving too fast
in a contrary direction.
I grasp the difficult mathematics of topology because I know
her saddle-shapes.
I know conic sections also from the fall of her skirt.
Transcendental numbers are not difficult since inside she is
much bigger than she is out.
As for theology, she always gives me good answers to my
short god.

VI COMING-LADY

She comes like a seashell without a skin,
She comes like warm mud that moves in sections.
She comes with long legs like a tree-frog clambering
Towards some great fruit, niddip, niddip.
A small acrobat lives inside her flower;
The canopy blooms.
She has an underground belfry tolling the bushes
Which shakes the ground,
It is full of shivering bats that fly out and return.
Her blouse comes off like the clean paging of new books,
There is a smell of fresh bread and a clean active
Strong-teated animal inside.
Her knickers come off like opening party invitations,
And between her legs pigeons are laying eggs without shells.
I have lost dread there longer than a man reasonably may,
I believe I know there white lids sledding over mossy wells,
Shearing prisms and silk splitting for me to walk
Into the red room in order to inspect the ancient portraits
In warm loose oils that are always repainting themselves.

SOME BOOKS, SOME AUTHORS, SOME READERS

There is dead wood in this author; open his book and certain pages crumble like rotten wood between covers of bark. Out of so much else scramble boot-shiny beetles, very compact and intent, like the readers it inspires, like the sincere readers of difficult dead books.

This one sloughs off his dead faces. They are the pages of his books. The old gentleman! – meet him now as pink and sweetly-smelling as a freshly-washed baby. A new book gathers in his face as we talk. He adjusts the shade of the club-room lamp so that it shines away from the darkness gathering in his face.

This one specialises in pages that become water as their white crests turn. Thus you can only read on, but there is a sea there containing many curious fish, and whales that move in schools together among their scented milt.

This one travels over sunlit waters in a shiny tin boat. He is very tanned, almost black, and sails with one hand grasping the white mast, but he cannot look down, the water is so bright.

This one writes books you do not read because they read aloud to you. Immersed in the writing, you lounge up to your neck in the talking water, your collar of water high around your neck, your river-robe fast-flowing.

The books of this one are like biting seaside rock. The same word runs straight through to the end.

This one makes books of stinking quicksilver. It is your own face you regard as you read, but the smell is the author's.

Opening the covers of this one's book is like opening a stove that has not been lighted for centuries. But its clinker is thousands of pearls.

How can I evaluate or describe to you the plots of any of these books, or the information they contain! For I am a lover of books, and this is my misfortune; to tell their worth is beyond me.

A PHILOSOPHY IN WELSHESE

The summer before last I saw my vision
Driving back from the cinema along the Pwllheli road
Having consumed no more than a quarter of Welsh whisky
Glancing out of my driver's window to the right

There was the vision walking over the sea
In a cloud of fire like raw tissues of flesh
Like an emperor bleeding at every pore because he is so alive.
On my left the sun westered behind the mountains
Which were dark and packed with too much scree,
Too many pebbles in slopes like millions of people

But on my right hand you walked over the sea in your single
scarlet garment!

I searched in my head for what you were called and I shouted
silently
OSIRIS or some such name and you wheeled slowly
Bowing to acknowledge my cry then as the road turned inland
The mountain got up slowly and laid along the crisp shore
Its pattern of farmers' fields that fitted each other endlessly.

Once there was this Chinese philosopher driving his horse and
cart
Through the mountain passes and he was not thinking exactly
of philosophy
His one thought was fuck the slut as he drove carefully along
the road towards her
Which concept alerted a nearby cloud that was coloured
exquisitely
Like blood washing away on a cool stream. The same cloud
Had been appearing nightly at this spot for six million years

Pondering over the pass in the ancient mountains without
hearing philosophy
Expressed with quite such concision and determination
before.

Brother! Old Friend! Colleague! I shouted to China.

This cloud rolled down the mountain like an immense
glowing dog
Followed him home and all night wrapped his house
As all night he fucked the slut and every night
People of the area observed that the sunset descended
To attend this holy man whom the gods kept safe.
He never understood why his reputation grew but he kept
hard at it
Preaching that if you wish to be loved by men of discernment
Find a slut and fuck her deep as she will go into her yin
Indulging your manifold perversions which you must woo
as a fair person
Which is what the Welsh whisky showed me and I wonder
whether it's true
On the road to Pwllheli driving back from the cinema at
Bangor
Through the great mountains on no more than a quarter bottle
taken
With Dante Alighieri, Charles Lutwidge Dodgson and Albert
Einstein in the back of the car.

SAM'S CALL

for Derek Toyne

My uncle Sam Lines always seemed
an enlightened person to me, but then I
was a child. I never went
to chapel where he preached, though people told me
he was a marvellous preacher. I asked him what he said:
he told me he never could remember.

He saw his double in the garden. Came in to my aunt:
I just saw a funny chap, an old un under the trees, he said.
All right, said my aunt. Went up to him
to take a closer look and it was me.

He had a lovely death. My aunt told me.
Almost gone, then up he sat, bolt upright and cried:
Meg lass, get me a clean shirt, I'll not be seen
dead in this one. They got him one,
struggled him into it, he never spoke again.

That was when I was guided, the one and only time.
Sam was laid out and waiting for his funeral.
I felt suddenly curious about an old box in the barn
Meg had said was full of old writings, now I must see them.
I went out quietly because of the death in the house
and the blinds down into the barn-smell
of chicken-shit and damp feed. Inside the box I found
one old piece of paper with green writing
'To be buried with Sam Lines,' folded,
a red mark and something stuck round and crinkled,
like an ancient condom, then the tears
spurted into my hand, I understood
it was his caul he had been born with.

He could tell the time without looking at his watch.
He'd sleep in his chair by the range; after supper
we kids'd creep up, whisper in his ear,
(head back and closed eyes fixed on the ceiling)
'Sam, what's the time?' His big oakapple hand
crept into his waistcoat, head still asleep
he took his turnip watch out and said the time
from his sleeping mouth. He was always right
you could check him from the watch his big hand
would close and tuck away into its pocket again.

DUNE-FIRER

Rocked with laughter, he is a Cornishman,
He says: 'There are no ghosts in England,'
Sand in the gold honey to chip your teeth on,
By the slipping sandhills, in his cottage window
Chewing his pipe, in his shirtsleeves, regarding
The crucifix of day and night, the beehives,
The bees buzzing, and the silent honey,
The painted signboard of the pub that shows
A man with flaming-torch-in-hand
Thrusting his light down a street that's sanded up.

Two stone benches in the church-porch
Two men opposite each other, dozing.
A gargoyle grips the full moon in its jaws.

He uncorked the Shrub bottle and poured me out
A cat's labyrinth of odours pacing round the garden,
A scent like a procession of scarlet judges
Their eyes closed.
                    'The Figure
Of the Saviour broke all the crosses.
Till my Grand-dad came with that stone
Or bone, you couldn't get a crucifix to hang.
The story has it they killed the saint
And his mother on the north beach
Where they were washed up in their tun-cask
At night, and light poured between the staves.
Greatly fearing they crept along the beams
Dazzled by the contents raised an axe
A voice cried – hold! and the iron bands
Sprang off with a chime and the barrel opened
Like a wooden flower, and sitting at its centre
Like stamens, pistil, the saint on his mother's lap,

Her golden breast spilling out of her gown
And he smiling up at them from his white meal.
And they smiled and laughed at the axe raised again
And the laughter went on as it fell splitting them,
And the light went out and the beach bubbled with blood.
The tide glowed and boiled as it washed the floor
So they said it must have been the devil.
And the axe was possessed with holy fear
And did it of itself. They say
That's how the stone was made
As lightning strikes the dunes and fuses sand
Their blood leapt like lightning around the beach.
One of my stubborn fathers cupboarded it in his cottage.
After that the Figure broke all his crosses.
Nothing went right until the bone came to the church.
You saw the figure on the signboard.
That was my Grand-dad in the village street.
The dunes were winning and he'd pulled that bone out,
The sand sprang and sprayed back before it,
The bone sang and the sand leapt back,
Something yelped and sprang into the sea
With a cliff of water as it plunged
And he walked straight up the churchyard-path
And the head-stones rocked and the coffins
Cracked underground like the resurrection
And he marched into the porch and put it up
On the shelf where it lies now, and they made
A little grilled door to keep it safe
And two men on duty all the time . . .

I think it's a bone out of a lizard's back
That walked the dunes two million years ago
And it's so peaceful with its years, it cures.
I've touched it to open-sores, and they scream
Like mouths, and having screamed
They close their lips for ever . . . I've had crab-lice

Run shrieking through the hair until they died.
The men like sitting there, because they dream
Great dreams they can remember, that are the bone's dreams,
Or their own dreams rising from the well of time-stillness
The bone makes in that porch, you'll feel it.'
We went through the church, past
Jesus hanging by his wounds in a blue sea-window
Over the altar; a side-window showed how
His head glowed like a thin gold cup
Under his halo as he wondered at his hand-wounds.
My friend nodded to his dozing mates,
Unlocked an iron grille in an inner pillar
Brought out the bone and touched it
To my tongue, I saw the scrotum delicately whorled,
The stout shaft resting, balls caught up in their skin,
I kissed the stone phallus, and he shut it away.

I wanted to ask him what he saw it as,
He thought it was a vertebra, a bit of a backbone,
But I saw it clearly . . . so did he. . .
And I felt the ulcer itching as it healed, I wanted to thank
But he interrupted: 'You're not finished.
It's cured your mouth. You'll not be finished
Till you come to guard here as well,
Not till you tear up your books
And come to read here with us in this porch
The book of dreams opened to us nightly,
The living book of scenes fresh-written nightly.'

TAPESTRY MOTHS

for Vicky Allen

I know a curious moth, that haunts old buildings,
A tapestry moth, I saw it at Hardwick Hall,
'More glass than wall' full of great tapestries laddering
And bleaching in the white light from long windows.
I saw this moth when inspecting one of the cloth pictures
Of a man offering a basket of fresh fruit through a portal
To a ghost with other baskets of lobsters and pheasants
nearby

When I was amazed to see some plumage of one of the birds
Suddenly quiver and fly out of the basket
Leaving a bald patch on the tapestry, breaking up as it flew
away.

A claw shifted. The ghost's nose escaped. I realised

It was the tapestry moths that ate the colours like the light
Limping over the hangings, voracious cameras,
And reproduced across their wings the great scenes they
consumed

Carrying the conceptions of artists away to hang in the woods
Or carried off never to be joined again or packed into
microscopic eggs

Or to flutter like fragments of old arguments through the
unused kitchens

Settling on pans and wishing they could eat the glowing
copper

The lamb-faced moth with shining amber wool dust-dabbing
the pane

Flocks of them shirted with tiny fleece and picture wings
The same humble mask flaming in the candle or on the glass
bulb

Scorched unwinking, dust-puff, disassembled; a sudden flash
                                        among the hangings
Like a window catching the sun, it is a flock of moths golden
                                        from eating
The gold braid of the dress uniforms, it is the rank of the
                                        family's admirals
Taking wing, they rise
Out of horny amphorae, pliable maggots, wingless they
                                        champ
The meadows of fresh salad, the green glowing pilasters
Set with flowing pipes and lines like circuits in green jelly
Later they set in blind moulds all whelked and horny
While the moth-soup inside makes itself lamb-faced in
The inner theatre with its fringed curtains, the long-dressed
Moth with new blank wings struggling over tapestry,
                          drenched with its own birth juices

Tapestry enters the owls, the pipistrelles, winged tapestry
That flies from the Hall in the night to the street lamps,
The great unpicturing wings of the nightfeeders on moths
Mute their white cinders . . . and a man,
Selecting a melon from his mellow garden under a far hill, eats,
Wakes in the night to a dream of one offering fresh fruit,
Lobsters and pheasants through a green fluted portal to a ghost.

THE SLEEP OF THE GREAT
HYPNOTIST

The sleep of the great hypnotist, who is underground,
Who is hypnotised on his monument with his stone book,
Who on his death-bed gave her a trance and into that openness
Dropped his posthumous suggestion, and died
As she awoke. Now she will never be free of him,
And it is night, and all the water speaks in his voice
Out of the springs under the pine-belts haunted by tawny
                                                    ghosts
(Great cheated hypnotists, the red owners of the land),
And now he with his spirit command has opened up this land
                                                    to her,
Her decent campus alive with the indecently dead, her father
Somewhere among them who has told her to dream of him
                                                    and shed
Spirit tears. The Indian Museum commands her to it
Where there are nose-bones, and painted sticks for the hair,
Effigy-pipes that are portable altars with a spirit to consult
That blows gentle blue whirlwinds from his carved-open head,
And there are skulls stained green from brass kettles in the soil,

And there are reindeer combs for causing dreams,
Cootie-combs to comb dreams into your hair before you sleep,
Gesumaria combs to comb fine orgasms into your hair;
And the dead Hypnotist's command unlocks this case with her
                                                    hand
And visions of running horses pass through her head
As his orders pass the comb through her mane. . .

Among all these Indians and knowledge where is her father,
Where, in this newly-alive world full of the dead?
A woman whose oily plaits shine in the starlight smiles at her:
'He is not born yet,' and pats her global tummy;

So she dreams of the great hypnotist among the Indian relics
By post–hypnosis after his death, and in the graveyard
The dead man tries to turn over one more page in his cold stone
book.

Over the dark snow, somebody throws a great window-spark
open

His last experiment wishes she were that squaw.

SERIOUS READERS

All the flies are reading microscopic books;
They hold themselves quite tense and silent
With shoulders hunched, legs splayed out
On the white formica table-top, reading.
With my book I slide into the diner-booth;
They rise and circle and settle again, reading
With hunched corselets. They do not attempt to taste
Before me my fat hamburger-plate, but wait,
Like courteous readers until I put it to one side,
Then taste briefly and resume their tomes
Like reading-stands with horny specs. I
Read as I eat, one fly
Alights on my book, the size of print;
I let it be. Read and let read.

The ghost that rapes, photographed suddenly on the stairs.
I see him climbing the stairs in flashes
I see him enter the bedroom in white flashes
In flashes he is unbuckling his workman's belt
He stands behind me in flashes as I write
I have risen from my bath and towelled myself dry
I am wrapped about in my clean towelling dressing-gown
I write about the ghost and he enters me in flashes
He sits in my clean body as on a human throne
I am the ghost who rapes who comes back for more
Who cannot rest because he cannot quite do it
I am the man who rapes, I have a ghost that needs to die
I seek the woman who will kill my ghost, she needs to be
                                              broken

The rain begins and each drop is charged with knowledge
There is the ghost who smiles in the river
And the ghost who eats dung because he is a mushroom
The ghost who eats corpses because she is grass
The ghosts which eat grass because they are beefs
The ghosts who are beefeaters because they are men
The ghosts who eat coal because they are flames
The ghost who rapes steps into my body
Newly-clean out of the quick flame of the candle into my body

He sits as on a throne in the slow flame of my body
The slow waxy flame of my body
The candle looks over my shoulder, my right shoulder, my
                                              left shoulder,
The candle creaks and spits and it says 'grease'
No it says 'ease' no it says 'jeeze' and very quietly 'us'
It eases us, peering over my shoulder
In the mirror, like the slant eye of a beast.

The shadows in the draught swirl about my head,
They are trying to wrench my face backwards
Into a ram's face with great horns of shadow,
A wise goat-face with a great muzzle, with moist nostrils,
With a little string of phlegm whipping in the left nostril
A ram's face with pupils of black stone and pleated gold foil
I raise the candle placing it between the goat's horns
Which are moons its flame like an eye open between moons
I ease you the lips of leather whisper I ease you
A little string of blood whipping in the left nostril.

A TWELVEMONTH

In the month called Bride
there is pale spectral honey
and in-laws made of chain-mail and whiskers.

In the month called Hue-and-Cry
green blood falls with a patter
and the pilchard-shoal flinches.

The month called Houseboat
is for conversing by perfume
and raising beer-steins:
great stone-and-foam masks.

In the month called Treasurechest
snails open jalousies onto their vitals:
pinecones, pollen-packed.

In the month called Brickbat
the sea is gorgeous with carpets
of orange jelly-fish squads:
and the people ride.

The month called Meatforest
is for flowers in the abattoirs,
catafalques for the steers.

In the month known as William
we watch the deer grazing on seaweed;
police open the strongroom of Christ.

In the month called Clocks
the poets decide
whether they shall draw salary,

And in the month called Horsewhip
they pluck their secret insurance
from the rotting rafters.

In the Mollycoddle month
barbers put up bearded mirrors
and no-one is allowed to die.

In the month called Yellow Maze
all the teddy-bears
celebrate their thousandth birthday.

In the month called Sleep-with-your-wife
the sea makes a living
along this quiet shore, somehow.

WHO'S YOUR DADDY?

(Ans.: 'H.M.S. Ark Royal!' – wartime joke)

I see a great battleship moored in the snow
I see the silvery pencils of guns that bristle
I remake this image, I try to,
It is a pine cone of lunar metal
Doors hinge in its steel, flakes fly,
Warm glows emerge
I see pollen
I see a pine cone consecrated to Attis
I see an ark
I know there are scrolls
Containing royal mysteries inside

Called explosives
Causing mysterious deaths understood by computer
It is a battleship
This will not be countermanded
It is a great battleship moored in the snow

It is not a white spider
Flying in its cracked web of the lake

It is not the discarded surplice
Of the summer-god, still warm inside

It is a battleship containing sailors
Trained to navigate and kill

It is no wedding-gown
Or wedding blouse with golden buttons
From which light shines across snowy sheets
It is no iced honey-cake of the sacrament of marriage
In which the honey is sweet light
That will last a couple of years
Of married breakfasts

It is a battleship

Commanded
Metal commanded
By a man with steel-ringed eyes
By a man with golden wedded cuffs
Under orders

It is no felled yule-log
Stuffed with presents
The honey-log of a sedated bear

It awaits orders understood by computer

It is the sledge made of dead men's nails,
The glittering horse of scythes,
The refrigerator of snowy carcases.

THREE AQUARIUM
PORTRAITS

(Penzance)

I

The lobster leans, and taps on the glass.
Among the fiery hands of light and ripple
It has a face like a barbershop of scissors
Shaving drowned men in a lambent steely light;
It has a face and shell
Of blue holly-leaves in a beating-gently breeze;
These details cleaning themselves always
Scissors through combs, and leaf rescrubbing leaf.

It walks like three headless armoured dancers
Of a machinetooled Masque of Industry
Who set their precision clawsteps down
With computered watery stilts on feathery ooze
That sends up gunpuffs. It sees
But it sees through sucked black stones on skinny telescopes.
Its swept-back aerials are the only red instruments.

It is *loppestre*, or spidery creature, but I dub it
Lob's Man, as a teamster gathers up his reins
Lobster has spikes and studs for harnessing to some evil,
Must be the jigsaw piece for some horn-hoof pattern
Being like a witch that marshlight blue
Carrying its hell's radio in those crimson aerials.
There! I can eat it with good conscience
Being our Lob-Star, the colour of Sirius,
Clanking on its platter, alive-boiled and buttered:
We shall eat the evil and make it our very own,
Cracking his male-claws with our silver pincers.

This is one picture along the dark corridor
Of windows like a train under the sea.
Instead of scenery streaming, flocks of birds,
We have the fishes who swim their little masks
Of innocence with big dark eyes in silver faces,
Of pouting generalship, decorated fins,
And nibble at her fingers, through the glass.
With ripples, dusky lights, these frames
Seem full, as the passage is, with fiery hands
That push out with other portraits, as
CUTTLEFISH AMONG GLASS-SHRIMPS.

III

The boots have golden eyes, like cats or sheep,
Slashed with a wavery iris, rippling welts.
They blush dark as fruitcake with a chewing beak
Deep in the centre of a flower of tendrils.
There is a creamy wand set in the moccasin
And when they slip upstairs as they like to do
Aiming this waterhose at their launching-pad
They are something between a pussy and a carnival-nose

Something between a fruitcake and a boot
A cross between a miniskirt and a pasty
Float water-gently like a gold-eyed turd
Of inscrutable wisdom among their glassy shrimps
High-stepping like lean assistants who are
Mainly spectacles and the joints of spectacles
Being entirely of glass with a few guts
But shining like a neon sign at every joint
Like ladders who are greenhouses and jobbing gardeners
Who are bees returning also, joints pollen-packed,
Easing their silver slivers like encased decisions
Of see-through steel whose clickering chimes
Bright-sparkle in water-sound, deafened by glass.

Among the always-twitching hands of fire
The creatures watch us, lobster
Ripped spiky from its pattern of imagined evil,
Precision prawns, those workers in glass,
And the biscuit-coloured, jet-propelled
And boot-faced cuttlefish.
They lean and tap the glass, and shiver
As we scratch back. To them
We are as they are, sea-creatures that float
With no support along the fiery corridors.
Through the glass
They wish to eat us, and turn us to themselves,
We lean back at them, our watery mouths
Like smashed aquaria with jagged fangs,
We return each others' looks among fiery hands.

ON LOSING ONE'S BLACK DOG

(An expression meaning 'to reach the menopause')

I

Thigh–deep in black ringlets,
Like a shepherdess at a black sheepshearing;
Like a carpentress in a very dark wood
Sawdust black as spent thunderstorms;
Like a miller's wife of black wheat
The stones choked with soot;
Like a fisherwoman trawling black water
Black shoals in the fiddling moonlight
Squaring with black nets the rounded water;
Like an accountant, knee-deep in black figures,
A good fat black bank balance in credit with grandchildren!
Tadpole of the moon, sculptress of the moon
Chipping the darkness off the white
Sliving the whiteness off the night

Throw down the full gouges and night-stained chisels!

Coughing black
Coughing black
Coughing black

The stained lazy smile of a virgin gathering blackberries.

II

We opened the bungalow.
The sea-sound was stronger in the rooms than on the beach.
Sand had quiffed through the seams of the veranda–windows.
The stars were sewn thicker than salt through the window
Cracked with one black star. A map of Ireland

Had dripped through the roof on to the counterpane
But it was dry. There was no tea in the tin caddy,
Quite bright and heartless with odorous specks.
There was a great hawk-moth in the lavatory pan.
Our bed was the gondola for black maths, and our
Breakfast-table never had brighter marmalade nor browner
                                                          toast.

Two ladies in a seaside bungalow, our dresses
Thundered round us in the manless sea-wind.
Her day-dress: the throat sonata in the rainbow pavilion.
We kiss like hawk-moths.

III EPHEBE

The beating of his heart
There was no translation

Eyes so round
The lad looked at me milkily

I had his confidence
In the dry street
Out came his secret

'The Battleship,' he said,
'We're going to see the Battleship'

As though a flower told me
Opened its deep pollens to me

He had teeth perfect and little as
Shirtbuttons, fresh and shining

He was about eight
Like a flower grown in milk

'The Battleship!' he said
So lively   supernatural
His soft thumbprint
Creeping among the canines

IV CRY JELLIES AND WINE

Preparing jellies and wines in autumn
Sad wife alone
The rooms golden with late pollen

The neat beds turned down
The children smiling round corners
Sweet-toothed, sweet-headed
Her fruit, her blueberries on canes

The sad wife who would not listen
Boiling jellies, filtering wines in autumn
What shall she tell the children

They will not listen
They love jellies, russet jams

The sad wife in autumn
Her jellies and wines stolen
Stolen by love, stolen by children

The rooms golden with pollen

V A VIBRANT WASP

A wasp hanging among the rose-bines:
Footballer wandering in an antique market;
Damask and ebony, mahogany thorns, greenglass rafters,
                                    veined parquets.

Again he struck the wasp with the sheets of paper and
Believes he kills it; the wasp
Clinging to the tendon of his ankle looked very sporting and
                                                        official
In black and gold clinging by the tail the high-pitched pain
Was yellow streaked with black oaths

He could not find the wasp-body it had been sucked
Along his nerves
                    after the rage
There is a sore pain turning to lust

That afternoon a plucky infant was conceived
Full of an infant's rage and juices
He struck once, and conceived

He struck at the wasp once, his child
Ran in out of the garden, bawling like a plucky infant
Teased beyond endurance in a striped football jersey among
                                            gigantic cronies.

VI THE STATUE OF HER REVERED
      BROTHER-IN-THE-BOAT

She catches the bloodless statue of her
Revered boatman-brother a ringing blow with
A mallet; the pure note vibrating
Through the gouged stone sustains
For three hours of morning reverie
During which time at this pitch
(*Om*) her petitions come to pass
Beyond her expectations, or anybody's:
                    gardens, walks,
Silvery lads and encounters among the knotgardens,
Clavichords humming to the shrill-chanting beds
In the manor dark as horn. Too soon
The singing stone falls silent and it is not yet time

To strike the next blow. Now that she has seen everything
It is time to strike the last blow, now that she has
Nothing further to ask, it is time to plead
That the rigid statue may grant its greatest boon and walk
As her living and immortal brother among
All the beds and garden beds and wives and grandchildren
Proved by the magic of her singing jewel; but first
Before he can so walk she must strike some blow,
The ultimate blow, the blow to end all blows

To finish things one way or the other, that will either
Reduce the great icon to bloodless rubble or
Free her brother to return
                                        rowing in
From the further shore: either
Make the wishing-stone alive in granting
The goal of bliss, or
                              shatter felicity, all.
                                                    (This blow
Is struck only by the lunatic when the moon is
Full and directly overhead and the stony particles
Aligned like the cells of a yearning throat
Ready to sing, the birth-passage of man-song
Through a woman-throat)

In the beginning it was violence only and the shedding of blood
That started the gods singing.

VII AT THE PEAK

The tables laid with snow
Spotless cold napery

Tense white snowmen
Seated on snowthrones
Knives of sharp water
Icepuddle platters

Iceflowers

Carving the snowgoose
Slices whiter than pages

The sun rises
The self-drinkers
Swoon under the table,

Glitter the mountain.
The rivers foam like beer-drinkers

Devising real flowers
And meat you can eat.

VIII THE TUTORIAL

My anointing
Gathers him
I draw the shapes of him
He has yet to learn
Over his skin
He recognises them

Flowing from feet to head
Baptism

He is a stony river, he swims with his head on the river
The brown body

I draw wings in the oil along his back
He is a youthful messenger

I anoint his chest
He is one of the facetious learned folk
Silky
It is my learning

I tweak his nipple
The county thunders
White oil
Displaces my
Black mirror.

THE TERRIBLE JESUS

It is the terrible Jesus
He walks on water because he hates its touch
He hates his body to touch everything as water does
(As Orpheus sang from the river of his body)
The ulcers close as he passes by
This is because he rejects ulcers
Anything raw and open, anything underskin
He rejects it or covers it with a white robe
He fasted forty days as long as he could because he hated food
And hated those who gave him food
And put worlds of feeling into his mouth
Lucifer came and tempted him out of natural concern
For this grand fellow starving in the desert
But would he pass the world through him
Like anyone else? Not at all.
He came back from the tomb because death
Looked like hell to him which is another thing
He won't do, die, not like everyone else.
Nor sleep with the smooth ladies.
Instead he goes up to heaven and hopes
For less participation there in those empty spaces
But from there he calls down to us
And I know those cries are calls of agony since there
All the sweet astrology-stars pierce his skin
It is worse than earth-death that destiny starlight for those
That won't join in, hedgehog of light.

This is the terrible Jesus. There is another,
And none will give him a name. He takes care.
He lives all around. I breathe him. He breathes.
Like the air we breathe, he is free to us.

THE VISIBLE BABY

A large transparent baby like a skeleton in a red tree,
Like a little skeleton in the rootlet-pattern;
He is not of glass, this baby, his flesh is see-through,
Otherwise he is quite the same as any other baby.

I can see the white caterpillar of his milk looping through him,
I can see the pearl-bubble of his wind and stroke it out of him,
I can see his little lungs breathing like pink parks of trees,
I can see his little brain in its glass case like a budding rose;

There are his teeth in his transparent gums like a budding
                                        hawthorn twig,
His eyes like open poppies follow the light,
His tongue is like a crest of his thumping blood,
His heart like two squirrels one scarlet, one purple
Mating in the canopy of a blood-tree;

His spine like a necklace, all silvery-strung with cartilages,
His handbones like a working-party of white insects,
His nerves like a tree of ice with sunlight shooting through it,

What a closed book bound in wrinkled illustrations his father is
                                        to him!

OR WAS THAT WHEN
I WAS GRASS

I was putting a bandage of cobweb on the sudden cut
In the pain the fly told me what the web was like
The spider's face with its rows of diamond studs
And my skin crackling as the pincers drove in
That crackling pain went all over me
I knew I would never grow well again, my shell crazed,
And the acid came from the jaws and began to turn me liquid
And I felt a terrible pressure all over with the suction
And I was drawn up through the tusks into that face.
Then I woke up as though I were in a distillery
Humming with energy, retorts of horn and transparent tubes
Buzzing with juices, but I was at rest
Sealed like wine in crystal vases, and I looked down myself
With my eyeskin which was the whole egg, and I felt
The wine condense and become smoky and studded with rows
Of the eyes through which I saw that the mother watched
Benevolently from the roof of the factory which was herself
And my father whom she had eaten was with me too
And we were many flies also contributing to the personality
Of the eight-legged workshop, and I began to remember the
                                                        man
I had fed on as a maggot or was that when I was grass
Or the snail slying from my shell crackled on the thrush's anvil?
And whenever my eyes closed or my shell crackled in pain,
It was as though I stepped out of black winged habits.

MY FATHER'S KINGDOMS

The lovely shimmering skins of water
Swooping between the lions
The gown of water of Trafalgar Square,
The hollow brides of water:
These belonged to my father;

And the policemen pacing it in their deep clothes,
Their silver switchgear on their Queen's helmets
They belonged to my father, said 'Good-day'

Saluting like the thunderous city.
All the clothes of the city-men, the umbrellas,
The sponge-bag trousers and the stiff white collars

Belonged to my father, the starched points,
The studs, the charged tie wedged in the points,
The sparkling shoes trotting down Threadneedle Street
Like city serge bright-sewing

These belonged to my father, and at the City's centre
God sat like a dome and with wide eyes
And broad wings and a smart tolerable beard
Jesus swam through St Paul's ceiling, said 'Good-day'

Saluting like the thunderous city
Which belonged to my father

The BBC's sparkling hair
Of lines of electricity that reached into our homes,
The voices that were correct from London

Belonged to my father
The trains belonged and the clocks obeyed the trains
And Selfridges and Father Xmas and Richmond Park
Belonged to my father, and his father gave it to him.

Even the bombs that fell on London
Belonged, he let a few in.

GOD SAYS 'DEATH'

God says 'Death' in a gentle voice
To the corpse sleepless with the wheats
That hiss on a low earth-note all night
Like a door hung over with dark leaves
Out of which the immense syllable blows:
'Death' in God's voice dressed in his spiderweb shirt
With its tassels of wheat, in his knobbly dressing-gown
Pulled from the oak; he
Says 'Death' with all his clothes,

And his mushroom buttons,
And his ponds which are mirrors
Tunnelling into the sky where he jumps up
Parting the thundercloud with electrical claws;

The reedy marshes of the railway, on some platform
Deep in East Anglia with the mire-drummer thumping
Through the lonely sky, God might pop out of the mud
Puffing a smoke rolled of flesh, dung and pelt,
And offer me one

And I could ask him then why 'Death',
And he would smile like a dago in his black cloak,
And offer me life to keep quiet about it,
'Would you Call God a liar?' he hands me flowers
From the churchyard: 'Do you call these dead?'

THE GRAND LUNACY

The moon is the mansion of the mighty mother,
With its one blazing window it wings across the sky,
It is the abyss, sensing everything,
It is the opener, pulling up the frail spirit,
Snapping its rootlets a little more, each time.

Its glassy beverage, sticky as libido,
Oozes out of the mistletoe,
My moon-yolk leaps out into the bedroom,
Moon-beam, self-coloured.

The dead are the embryo people of the earth,
They are called Demetrians, eternal freshness
Is guaranteed for them; as the moon passes
They all stand on tiptoe, her beams
Comb them, they are like cobwebby wheat
As the wheat is, with its indefinite stalks,
Its frayed alleys of shadows, bending, tiptoe.

It is she who causes the woman's tongue in my mouth
To branch like an antler, and the wings of cupid
Deep in my body, to beat; it is she
Who twines her fingers in my skin,
Flays a layer as one pulls
A sheet off a mirror in which she stares

From the one window flying in the sky of her stone cottage.

SEAN'S DESCRIPTION

The grave of the careless lady who swallowed pips,
From the rich subsoil of her stomach and snapped coffin-timbers
A fine greasy crop of apples glittering

With their waxes; and Sean told me
Over a customary glass the best description he'd read
Of what a dead person looked like, actually:

'A green doughnut with eyeholes in it,' he said,
'A green doughnut with black cream,' as we sat

By the waterlilies rooted in mud of the pub garden,
And a bumble-bee in a tippet of glossy fur
Snatched a line from the air, and I brought
One of her apples from my pocket, and bit
Through the sweet flesh that fizzed with young ciders
And my toothmarks blazed white through the red skin.

'Look,' I said, holding up another firm sweet apple,
'This is what a dead person really looks like; taste her.'

PLACE

The train's brakes lowing like a herd of cattle at sunset
As it draws up by Lesson's Stone, by mountains
Like deeply carved curtains, among small birds
Knapping at the stationmaster's crumbs, hopping-black
Like commas of wet ink: I could see their small eyes glisten.
I thought I must die in my sleep, I lay in my bunk
Like wet clothes soaking, the convulsions were the journey,

The bedroom bumped. I stepped off and the mountain landscape
Was like stone guests set round a still table
On which was set stone food, steaming
With the clouds caught on it; a plateau
Surrounded with peaks and set with cairns
And stone houses, and a causeway up to Giant's Table,
And the railway trailing like a bootlace. My house
Was hard by Lesson's Stone, near the sparkling Force
That tumbled off the cliff, that in summer
Left its dry spoor full of thornbush. Then the lizards
Flickered among the rocks, like shadows
Of flying things under a clear sky, or like
Bright enamelled painted rock on rock, until they swiftly
Shot sideways too fast to see. I arrived
On Lesson's Stone Stop platform a decade ago;
The place where I live is still like pieces
Of a shattered star, some parts shining
Too bright to look at, others dead
As old clinker. I am afraid to mention
The star's name. That would set it alight.

The pornographic archives guarded by bees
Who have built comb in the safe; iron doors
From which the honey drips; I sip a glass
Of bee-sherry, yellow and vibrant; I came here
Past the old post-office, boarded up,
From within the cool darkness sun-razored
I heard the hum of bees; my friend tells me

That the radioactive cities of the future
Will be left standing for euthanasia,
They will be kept beautiful though all trees
And lawns will be plastic. Those who wish to die
Will drift through the almost-empty streets,
Loiter through the windows of the stores,
All open, all untended, what they fancy they can take,
Or wander through the boulders of Central Park, its glades
To hear the recorded pace and growl in the empty zoo-cages,
And consider the unperturbed fountains of water,
While it, and they, are rinsed through and through
As the pluming spray by sunlight, with killing rays,
Lethal broadcasts, until they can consider no more.
Germs over the whole skin die first, the skin after,
Purity first, then death, in the germless city that amazes
The killed lovers with its pulsing night-auroras.

I reply I would prefer a city constructed of OM,
A city of bees, I want this disused city
Converted to a hive, all the skyscrapers
Packed with honeycomb, and from the windows
Honey seeping into the city abysses, all the streets
Rivers of cloudy honey slipping in tides,
And the breeze of the wings as they cool our city.

This would be my euthanasia, to be stung by sweetness,
To wander through the droning canyons scatheless at first,
Wax thresholds stalagmited with honey-crystals
I snap off and munch, and count the banks
That must brim with the royal jelly . . .

And some wander through the sweet death, city of hexagons
And are not stung, break their hanging meals off cornices
In the summer-coloured city, drink at the public fountains
Blackened with wings drinking, and full of wonder
Emerge from the nether gates that are humming
Having seen nature building;
                                        others stagger
Through the misshapen streets, screaming of human glory,
Attended by black plumes of sting,
With a velvet skin of wings screaming they're flayed.

A great longhaired hog, glistening with the dew,
It knows night by heart, sucked through blue irises,
But day it allows to rest and glitter on its skin
And its long hairs harsh as fingernails
Like coarse reeds on a hump of the bog.
It is a golden pig and its underslung rod
Is the very word for *thrust*, like the drill
Into the future, and it will run along that drill's sights;
But now, glistening with distillate, it waits
For the sun to raise moulds of steam along its back,
For the sun to warm it dry and the air to towel it
Testing its hooves meanwhile that clock on the stone,
Ready with its seed and tusks and bolts of muscle
And the grease of seed it pumps into the black sow
Like lightning-bolts into the hulking black thunder anvil
And the storm will gather until it breaks and rains pigs,
The mud glorious with rain-shine, pig-grease and wallow.

LIVING IN FALMOUTH

I

Seagull, glittering particle, climbing
Out of the red hill's evening shadow into sunslant
At high tide and sunset; there is a moth
On the rusty table that spreads out wings
Like lichened tombstones.

A crackwillow leaf
Floats into an ashtray; we are among mirrors

And water, and the small windowed boats
Gently in the tide play with long beams
Like silent swordplay

And the gull arrives into the high air
Still full of sunshine, and his particle shines

And the boats knock gently among the shades
And the heads nod

And the good and bad dreams come swimming
Up out of the water glittering as they arrive

Sliding from under the red hills on which
The four-legged phantasms of wool graze,

Cloud-dreams let loose a moment of shower,
Dream-tides knock the fencing dream-boats
And two-legged dreams make one flesh.

I sit inside one of her granite tents
Praising against reason the high winds,
The stars hard like gimlets, her bronchitis,
Her onset of winter and damp moulds,
Her spooks that do not linger,
Her magic touches.

She is only the same town from day to day
In the sense that a book is the same from page to page:
Or her water in the estuaries banked high
With mica-mud that glistens like satin garments
Ready for the spring to put on and shake out
To every colour, is the same water
That lies glowering under corpse-skies.

The tourists run like tides through granite houses,
Their ebb the dereliction of seaside pavilions,
Summer woods like smashed clocks, cliffs
Like crumbling cloudscape, dry-rot like wood-spooks
With white cobwebby arms: a bad smell, holding
Out a large repair-bill. Falmouth's bathing-beauties
Are sewing next summer in their dressmaking classes,
Her art-school a tenement of night-dreaming canvasses;
His clouds a tight lid God fastens on the box
Full of thousand-year-old churches and stony boarding-houses
Deciduous of visitors; her echoing mines
Terrible art-galleries for works
Of miner-death that mills tinfoil, of cars in the raw
Bleeding over the roofs of profound caverns. That
Organ-note as the Redruth wind blows over the moor
Winds on the pipes of long-dead mines,
Brings all the bad weather, all the 'flu.

This is the wind that blanches Falmouth, shrinks it
To thin-glassed tombs of drunken landladies;
Her blossoms wither, like an alcoholic flush;
The tourists ebb like tides out of the houses.

I V

Falmouth water like a seven-fingered hand
Flat on the land. We have early elephant,
Bear, ox-ancestor and deer. The deep creeks
Were communication lines between hill forts
Where the hairy matriarchs crept for cover. We escaped
The shunting glaciers that streamed across Europe.
There was a language, part Celtic and part Latin;
A sell-out to the God quartered at Exeter;
A religious college in low woodlands
Near the head of Penryn river; and a chain-boom
Across the creek in the name of St Boudicca.
Until our first-born comes I am an invader.

v

Sun steers from the muddy Falmouth east
And docks above Swanpool, the air clears,
The sun's great hull lies above us, it is time,
Which is a red-hot hull. The great sun-sailors
Take liberty and stroll about the town,
The drawing-rooms expand as they peep in,
The hills are emerald and the cliffs sheer gold.
Their leave is short. They one by one ascend
The shrinking ladders of the dusk
Into the smaller, redder, westering boat. Shall we board
Into the night? To a man we have a ticket.

V I

A ship's figure-head bobbing in on the tide?
A floating pew, shaggy with saints?
Then I saw some of the hair was roots, it was an oak
Upended, a tree swimming ashore.
It bumped against the quay, nobody I could see
Stepped off its felloe of roots, but the town lightened
As if this traveller had tales. Two hundred years
Of voyaging oak, by its girth; say it had sailed
Round the world upsidedown since Garrick cast
An acorn into the Thames from Parliament Bridge. We got a
                                         tractor
And wrapped chains and lugged it from the harbour,
The gears screamed with the weight of the wet leafhead
Spread through the harbour like a green medusa
Dragged out of the sea full of acorns and foliage
Encaching tons of brine. I think the rains had clawed it
Out of Trelissick's precipitous shores upriver;
The Clerk replanted it in our Gardens. In my dreams
It is a true sea-oak, riding shockhaired over the dark water,
Voyaging through the years white-barked like moonlight,
Its branches like veins of light dredging the deep.

V I I

The whole world's water at some time or another
Flows through the Carrick Roads, bringing
Its memories and Chinamen, its Portuguese ships,
Its sectarians and its briny sea-fruit.
Some days the water is bloodstained with trade-battles,
Others it is birth-water running like hot fat,
Sometimes it is industrial dregs, quite often
It runs pure from crystal springs:

And Helford oysters
Sit in the Passages selecting these waters.
Harvested by leathery faces with good eyes
And hands like watercourses, they entrain to London,
To the potted ferns and bow ties,
Where they induce savoury dreams of moonlit water
And Ancient Cornwall, in new young tycoons,
Seductive Poldark dreams that draw the money west . . .

We watch the great cars glide by to the boardrooms,
We own only topsoil, the minerals are reserved,
The ground is sold under our feet.
The Oysters call them here, the Blooms keep them.
They will own everything. Let the land
Packed with underpalaces of gold dripping with oil
Be oyster-tales only, told to a mining penis
On a hotel-bed in London; let it be rumours only, lest all
Our first-born be made miners by the great absent landlords:
Not made deep starved miners by the enormous absent
landlords.

V I I I

The old intelligent villagers, the brilliant old village
Studies at the Open University over the antique wireless in the
kitchen;
George the Cowman crosses the Tamar to get his degree next
Tuesday:
He will be a physiologist with cross-fertilisation in economics.
Meg who milks has a doctorate in the Botany of Byres.
Carpenter Joshua studies Geology which is what his trees
grow from:
How the rock grinds into green wood which planes and
seasons accurately!
Jack Dustman carries books into the house bin-secretly, and
reads Bones.
Baker Jones spells out Philosophy in the light of his red ovens.

Cinder-cakes and sour beer. In the cider-cellar,
A corner stuffed with cobwebs, and a little grey drinker.
He drinks and drinks until his loins hurt, and what does he see?
It is what he thinks he thinks that matters to him now.
He thinks of all the stars like animals, he thinks he dreams
He snips a piece of bristling fur from each, and puts
Peltry of light into his purse to sew a suit from.
He jerks awake and laughs, in his cider-cellar corner.
When he tries to tell us about it, he gets lost
Among the procession of animals, and animal-headed men,
In among the feet and hooves plashing starlight. Amazed,
I suppose, like him, I love the moist stars of morning:

Orion with his brilliant cock shining like the wet spiderweb,
Like a ladder of light heavier than all the world,
Climbing in his drenched plumage like pulsing snow,
Like a silver beaten so long that it gives back light in pulses,
Or like a black tree over-arching, of white apples with pulsing
                                                              juice,
Or like a rainfall so massive it gluts and cannot fall,
Or like a full-rigged black ship, sailing with all knots white,
Or like wet herringbones at the rim of a great black plate,

Or am I drunk on apples like crushed stars, potent fruit,
That turns you grey and folded one day as cellar spiderweb?

X

Our radio is sensitive, but there is, thank God,
Beethoven sunlight beaming from the ionosphere,

Yet I can hear rain on the radio, and I think I can hear
The sheep tangled on the hillside, and I'm pretty sure
I can hear the broad black stairs of the slate quarry
Like pages torn out of the open hillside
Rustling packets of static;

And there is thunder! far distant,
High-pitched, like cellophane;

The soft grey sacks of rain pass over
In scratchy slippers,
The water is a continual whisper
That paces all ways down out of the skies,
Plashes on boulders, puts itself together
In new ways, raising rain-smells
Over the boulders, down from the moors;
You can hear every rasp and scratch
Of water from our speaker,
Every drop in the whole sky:

And Beethoven's gone, dead
And buried in busy Cornish water.

X I

Sea-waves that are dry
Come off the tide
Or off the rolling Redruth highlands,
Electrical Winds,
Charging us up

It is one explanation.
Waves of exhilaration,
Waves of political rich broadcasts put out by the moorsoil,
Sparkling their invisibilities, recharging us.

The real broadcasters are marching, they are a sightless surf,
There is wave after wave of imperceptible police,
Invisible black psychiatrists in coats the colour of sea-wind,
Invisible white healers in the moonlight
Charging us up

The gusty weather heaves all the leaves of the brain,
The red cells scatter, you can see views through them,
We shall be down to the skulls soon –
Recharge us!

The dead have powerful lungs,
Lungs like parks, sky lungs,
The cemetery sex-adepts at their pursuits,
Joining the worlds with their maggoty electricities,
They set my mind to work with poisoned arrows
That dance you to death like windy trees
Charging about.

From this room we see a clock of breeze
And clouds that run fast or slow depending on
How much we interest each other,
Recharging ourselves

Great dockleaves stampeding in veridian pelts,
Herds of them with muscles of breeze,
Leathery resurrectionists!
The dew crackles and sparks,
Charged up,

In this wind the Goddess kisses every child at once.

XII

The church is very real, absolutely too real,
It is realer than me, realer than where I live;
If this church is a house then I am a white shadow;
Look, there are written stones here 200 years old.
Being my senior by 200 years they do not speak to me,
Except with formal cursive manners like engraved visiting-cards
Quoting their names and numbers, their vast antiquity.
They are so still my footsteps must fidget them,

I expect they wish I were as still as they are,
Sitting in some pew studying stoniness until I grow slatey-cold.
And there is that vast cross-death that is worshipped inside,
Tainting the air with sweats and hymns so that breath,
Which is something he doesn't need on his side of the altar,
Is like a superfluous whispering of trees, appropriate to trees
Which are best cut down and employed as crosses,
Or chilled till they turn to stone; this death
Is so vast and old that the local deaths are trivial,
The people of the stones have not died, they have moved into
the yew-shadow,
Which is a tree that has been casting shadows longer than I
have,
And my parents who cast me are moving into the shadow: I
follow slowly.

AMONG THE WHIPS
AND THE MUD BATHS

She offered the liqueur glass of Grenadine
Between her legs; the beard lapped it up;
She swooned, recovered, said
M. Grenadine's the man for me; and from that day
The establishment was known as Mme. Grenadine's.
I saw her lose her temper with a punter once.
It was unprofessional, but after forty years of coaxing old
cocks

She thought she had a flier, and it was not.
She screamed at him so furiously the sparks of anger
Danced in her teeth, picking them; she had a mouth
Of blue flame; I *think* I saw this; I was so respectful
That when she blew her top like Krakatoa I saw things
I did not believe. This went with the rumours of China,
How she was said to have learned to ease the slow blue
lightning
Out of her skin and out of her lover's skin

So that they were sheathed in radiance, and the dark room
Flickered with their body-prints, like sand-dunes electrified
After a dry day. I did go in without knocking once
And I saw something gleaming, but it was so faint,
A kind of mouldy shine on the snoring bodies
Wrapped like beached tunny in their silken sheets.

I have flickered static out of the great bed
Its sheets clung to me and would not be smoothed,
And there is continual restless bedmaking in this place, but
aside from that

Her power makes me see things, I mean her personality, I
                                      mean my love,
Among the balustrades and carved galleries of her house,
The damasks and the fur rugs, the whips and the mud baths:

All that sex populates my imagination and makes me happy.

THE WEDDINGS AT
NETHER POWERS

I

The grass-sipping Harvestmen, smelling
Like haylofts on stilts, creaking
Like wet leather; a raven hops
And picks at them through the gravel:
It has macabre dandruff.
In its spotted froth the bark-faced toad squats
Among the daffodils like Stars of David.

II

A wasp crawls over the crucifix, sting out
Searching for a vulnerable part; the savage vicar
Strikes, the usurper bursts in melted butter
And horn-slices; another takes its place
Searching with its sting out over the holy places.

III

A gold-and-black body pinned to a matchstick cross,
The extra leg-pair free, glossy with wax, their cloven
Dancing-pumps shadow-boxing with slow death;
The sting stretched out in agony and clear drops
Slipping along the horny rapier to the tip
Where a woman crops the venom in an acorn-cup.

IV

The laboratory with skylights, the glass assemblies,
Tubes, taps, globes, condensers, flasks and super-hot flames:
With windows wide open to the pouring waterfall
White with every colour and exclaiming with every word,
With roof wide open to the starfall; just down the stream
The Mud Shop, with fifty-seven varieties of bath.

V

Two birds singing together like learned doctors;
The dew is open on every page;
He washes the dog's feet gently with warm water;
She spreads luminous marmalade on cindered toast;
There is no tree of flies in which creamy skulls lodge,
$$\text{humming,}$$
No dogs here have intercourse with any virgins;
There is a slug in the garden grey as a city kerbstone;
There is a cool sweet book of one page bound in appleskin.

V I

One hundred ship-weddings, the scoured planking, the pure
$$\text{sails,}$$
The bride's train blazing across the scrubbed poop,
The century of marriages and a hundred brides
Pulled over the water by their blinding veils.

The cool tankard engraved in wriggle-work.
A slight scraping or nibbling noise
In the house-timbers, like boughs chafing.
The salmon-silvery river over the red rocks.
A clockwork theatre. A munumental
Calendar musical longcase bellows-clock,
That measures the lunations and strikes
Christmas again after thirteen have passed.
A salt-saw in a glass case over the fireplace.
Rev. Uncle's 'Obby 'Oss: the rotary spark discharger,
Stinking of ozone with the blue crackling spark
Leaping among its wires like a chattering monkey.
He says: 'Teeth are the most indestructible of fossils,
And I wish to understand everything to understand God,
And because it is Sunday I make electrical sparks
To remind me of His Holy Ghost, nut-cracking ape
Swinging from Apostle to Apostle chattering
In tongues. I make myself
Both literate and numerate, Peter, and the alphabet
Is God's knucklebones of Pentecost
Where he fleshes himself fingers of flame, my lover,
And in algebra numbers are letters, you can hear
God's voice of creation when you vibrate the equations . . .'
And he did so, singing quadratics,

'Let X be middle C: now strike me an A . . .'
And I did so, on the piano.
'Not that the fossil-stone is a shut-in god,
Say rather it is a constant, something so slow
It shows its godlikeness only by residence
In many centuries. Don't tell the Bishop
But God-Mumgod made the world in their image;
Virgins like you will understand in due time . . .

Ma–God is a sea-maid, created from brine
Delicate skinned patterns of beating gonads
Like a fleet of umbrellas frailer than rain
Each like a seawater castle or mandala
A curtained pulse of bliss of the sea
And I tell you, boy, being dead is like that,
A celestial jellyfish shaped like the sky, beating, beating,
A whole eye, grazing on aether . . . but I love
Being God's vicar on two legs, lad, and the hymns,
Give me that A again . . .'

In my Uncle's library, my Mother's brother,
Every book and stone after church
Speaking his tongue, and on the brass lamp
His dog-collar swinging like a starched half-moon.

THREE-HUNDRED-YEAR
MOMENT

for G.M.

See the skeleton
And thou seest Death;
See the interior of the skeleton
And thou seest the Awakener.
The smoke motionless over the bonfire,
Cerebral enfilades; the fire has stopped to watch itself:

The beetle on the consuming leaf
Continues feeding
Among the stiff, hindered flames.
Who can tell
When the smoke
Will begin rolling again
When the flames
Will leap into their fiddle again, and eat?
Now they are like coiled shells,
Rosy with light, with fringes
A little stained with grey, like a cluster
Of shells of yellow and purple
Tied with ribbons of smoke;

I am a bouquet, says the fire,
With a grey hood, like a monk,
At this speed – but I am

At my fastest a bomb-blast,
And I am everywhere, in fact, says the fire,
This pile of leaves or that candle or that filament
Make me visible, that is all,

Let the bouquet live dangerously fast,
I mean the one in her hand, and she loses
The hand in a flash; let the grass
Live at the speed the sun burns
And we are dead in an instant;

And the trees, the grey volutes
Lope away over the red-hot fence,

Or stand for a three-hundred-year moment.

ON THE PATIO

A wineglass overflowing with thunderwater
Stands out on the drumming steel table

Among the outcries of the downpour
Feathering chairs and rethundering on the awnings.

How the pellets of water shooting miles
Fly into the glass of swirl, and slop

Over the table's scales of rust
Shining like chained sores,

Because the rain eats everything except the glass
Of spinning water that is clear down here

But purple with rumbling depths above, and this cloud
Is transferring its might into a glass

In which thunder and lightning come to rest,
The cloud crushed into a glass.

Suddenly I dart out into the patio,
Snatch the bright glass up and drain it,

Bang it back down on the thundery steel table for a refill.

THE BRITISH MUSEUM
SMILE

None of the visitors from teeming London streets
Smiles. The deeply-lined downtrodden faces
Elbow the galleries. The sphinxes inside smile
And the colossal faces.
The face of a king with shattered legs
Smiles. And the guards smile. Their solitude
Forms into a smile and the patience
Of all the seated faces in navy uniforms
On the little chairs with the deeply-marked cushions
Smiles. They have caught it from the sphinxes
And the colossal kings and the powerful scribes
With the stone incense-bowls who smile sweetly
Over the smoky crowds. Some of the smiles
Are printed on the air from the faces of the guards,
And the stone faces have dissolved a little in the air;
Passing through and through the smiling galleries
Rubs inch by inch the face into a smile,
The smile of the king you pass (whose legs are sand),
The imagined absent smiles of the drenched nereids
Whose headless robes blow back against their flesh
In many folded smiles, whose smiling heads
Are museum air; the mummies
With their gasping toothy grins
Under the polite smile-paintings of their coffin-shells
Lumbered here by ship and block and tackle
Scattering a trail of smiles; elsewhere
The nereid heads are pebbles or sand,
And who picks up the pebble smiles at its smoothness;
(And the sleek sand is made of microscopic nereid heads
Turning and kissing in the water of the tide
The smiles rubbing from quartz lip to lip,
Dissolving in the sea and flying on spume;

The mariners inhale, and smile.)

Such smiles have flittered down
Like pipistrelles of Egypt on to the faces of the guards
And the smiling guards know something unknown to their
                                                    crowds,
Something fallen from the sphinx that patters down
To fit you as you sit still on a stool
Polishing with your back those polished stones
For twenty years, or among those polished volumes
Not reading, but learning that smile. It took
Four thousand years to teach that smile
That flutters in these galleries among the guards
Who exchange mirrored smiles across glass cases; how
Did stone first catch it, that virus smile?

MY FATHER'S SPIDER

The spider creaking in its rain-coloured harness
Sparking like a firework. In the cold wind
Round the sharp corner of the house,

In the cold snap of that wind,
Many turned to ice:
Circular icicles.

My father lifted one off
Very carefully over the flat of his glove.
When I see these hedgerow webs

It is always with the sighing of the sea
In my heart's ear; it was at the seaside
In the smell of sand and tar that I first

Understood the universal perfection
Of these carnivorous little crystals
Coiling from their centres like the shells.

They were cruel and beautiful
At the same time; abominable
And delightful; why else did the silly

Flies dart into them to be drunk
Up like horny flasks, as if
The pints of beer had veiny wings –

If I could see those dartboard webs
Surely they could. They are doorways
To death and the mandala-sign

Of renewed and centred life. And this one,
Here, look, with its array of full lenses
(For the thread is fine enough for minutest

Beads to catch and roll the light in strings)
Is like a Washington of the astronomers,
Planned, powerful, radial city, excited by flying things,

At every intersection and along each boulevard
Crowded with lenses gazing upwards, pointing light.

DELIVERY HYMN

(During birth the baby's head rotates against the os crucis *at the back of the mother's pelvis.)*

See! the Woman is coming,
A Christ child in sun's rays
Painted across her clothing.

The Ancient of Days is in His heaven,
Dangling like a parachutist in angelic cords
Among white wings feathering and beating;

The Ancient's finger is hushing His nose,
He is white-nightied in womb-clothes,
Curled currents of birth-water are His beard;

His Mother's true presence rustles through all her veins,
He knows the whole Torah,
His skull bowed and in the mouth the small thumb,

Preaching the thumb-suck sutra from the hollow womb.
See, under her bellyskin little knuckles punch up at heaven!
The Mother croons over her cathedral-dome

Hymns to her Ancient who will emerge into light and form
Fragrance and other wonders in His good time,
But is first to be crucified headlong on bone.

Now He is full-bearded and in the nave,
His serene locks are curled pulsations of the water,
He is warm-shirted in membrane,
And knows the whole Torah.

(The Woman is coming now, and some Christ spills
Bright-red over her clothing.)

THE SIRE OF BRANCHES
AND AIR

———————

I

The sire of branches and air.
The low waters begin
To give off their cunny smell;
It means rain is near.

We have the emergency edifice,
The umbrella, which is a cross
Between a city suit and an office.
The moist wind bends the trees

Which have acquired presence
And their extra dimension
From this alluring smell
Forced through their budding branches

From hammered reservoirs like cold pewter shields
To which they add their own pinch of cunning.
They are threads of pulse
To which the breeze

Puts its own beating fingers
Gently, like a bearded physician.

II

The branches toss with such question,
And swell with such abandon,
I think each tree is a child at play,

It has donned the wind
Like a playsuit that thinks up games,
And falls thoughtfully into its quiet folds,

Then the resumed wind mounts
The stiff sire of branches,
It is a ghost trying on bodies,

Streaming over the land and letting them drop
After their battles.
A great face opens laughing

In that tree-head, and in that other
Head, the hair smarms flat as a seal.

I think that elsewhere this spectre also
Is a child; that somewhere in a nursery
Just over the treetops, a child's

Sleeping body lies in its white bed,
Emptied of the small omnipotent ghost
That can overturn a countryside

Of leafy timbered rooms, like a burglar
Passing invisibly through green walls;
Now large pawmarks appear printed

Across the leafhead and satisfied
The spirit of the child condenses
From the muscles of wind,

Lays itself along the little body and
Shrugs its way back into the angelic countenance.
I open the nursery door on my way to bed,

There is a knowledgeable smell of rain;
I shut the window and notice how still
The cunning trees are on the ridge after the storm.

EARTH SHAKES AWAY ITS DEAD LIKE CRUMBS FROM A CLOTH

They have smoothed their mounds down,
The dead, they have healed the soil and gone;
All is smooth lawn, a trifle long.

Where there was once an orchard of stone,
They have left, however it was done,
Only a seeding lawn, a trifle long

That works in the wind like television:
Across grass pictures, viewless sprinters run,
The prints of an invisible force flying,

Every wing-beat distinct in the grain
Of winnowing stalk and shadowing stem.
They have picked up their skeletons,

The people of clay, they have walked in their bones,
Plucked up their gravestones and not scythed the lawns;
I cannot tell how it was done;

All vanished into grass, a little long.
They have pulled up their static stones,
Their texts, and tucked them under their arms,

They have gone off like borrowers in the evening,
In the twilight returning dull thick tomes;
I wish I knew how it was done,

The graven texts gone.
All that is left is a shivering lawn;
Under it I can't tell where who was lain,

Or whether or how he is coming again,
The writing gone. Shadows hunt on the wind,
Calf-deep in cool grass I could hardly be stung

By these shadows of snakes, by these skimming scenes
Healed into a park; my feet laved in soft grasses
I wade through green streams.

Where are they hiding? I want to meet them
Now, before they are departed and quite gone.
Will they not be clean

And cool, like this wind-driven lawn,
And like the wind flying into the unknown,
Not by still text kept down, or solemn stone?

ROCK, EGG, CHURCH, TRUMPET

There is a churchy rock
Mothy with seagulls
Looking as it would fly

If only they would beat together
Their bread-mould pinions,
Fly like an angel of rock

With a stubble of wings;
Ripples pass over the rock
As though it were planted thick

With wheat that is mouldering.
The gulls mew-mew.
The rock that has indeed become a church

Is crazy with its wounds,
Having been sliced from the hill and
Blown up from it, and fitted together

On the same hill, a little higher:
The windows moan, the hinges shriek,
It is carved into weeping angels, it is

Thickly-set with their wings and open-mouthed guttering,
And is something between an egg and the rock;
Church is one of three kinds of feathered stone

That cannot fly. An egg is full of feathers,
A sealed stone globe, the pebble of a bird
That has roosted and will roost on a grey rock

That ripples its hide with feathers and shadows
In the creaming tide; and the church
Bellows with song attempting to take off

With the hymning engine of pewed people
Throbbing to us across the waves.
Stone is not just such an inertia –

Look at the little gymnast
Swinging to music along parallel bars
On those long bones; listen to the Tibetan

Flute of bone and the shoulder-blade violin
Strung with gut, and the creamy violin
Held high in the claws of a feathered angel;

The stone moon carved with a hare
Swoops over the feathering sea
That beats like the one tidal wing of the world –

Pull the cold bone up to your lips, Trumpeter,
Bark out with your angel-breath laden with spirits!

FROM THE LIFE OF A
DOWSER

Water is bad for him, much too exciting.
He runs away to Cornwall and drinks
From the sparkling well, *Fenten ow Clyttra.*

As he lifts the tin cup he wonders,
Trembling like the water in the cup,
What it will show this time, after so long,

They have boiled his water, made him drink tea,
That is stunned water, but he believes it thinks
As it tumbles over rock, breaking white,

Or streams into the high air, breaking white,
Or lies below its lintels in old stone wells
Pondering like some long transparent god

Waiting to be consumed and joined to more of him.
The Dowser believes, looking into his cup
Where air-bubbles in the water cluster

On sheer mirrors like silver tods of grape
And feels like that god about to drink
Some vineyard that is moonlit. He shuts his eyes,

The water is cool, and tin-tasting,
A spectre of earthy darkness brushes by
His throat, and disappears. There is nothing more.

He gets up from his knees and brushes them, regards
The avenue of long grass in which he stands

That burrows into the hillside with at its end
The stone lintel to water like an open wardrobe
With clothes of light flung about the grass

The dew-sheen and the spidery coronets
Which shiver like those bubbles of the well,
And a triple stone head on the cross-beam leering.

Still nothing more. Maybe this
Is enough to dig a well into the hill for,
To sculpt it and process, to make pilgrimage,

But then, why here, when everywhere
I break some slate in a damp cutting and water springs,
Whenever I dig my garden down into the water-table,

Prod five finger-freshets in the ferny turf.
Water is everywhere, and I think with it,
And remember with it, inside this rock

(And raps his knuckle on his brow),
And speak with it, as the clouds make scenes
And scrolling pictures, like a god

Opening his mouth and bellowing through
Lips and beards of water, water streaming
Through him like a fall or force, when

The frowning clouds in white coats came for him
Like falls walking and he forgave them. Now water
Is still in him, and well, and pondering.

RENFIELD BEFORE HIS
MASTER

(Renfield was the lunatic in Dr Seward's asylum who assisted Count Dracula during his English expedition, and who loved to eat flies.)

I

He was eight when he started earning
His living in a silk factory;
The big bales, corded with twist,

The incipient peignoirs, the feminine slink.
Was he a spider at all, once?
The managing director nipped the nub

Of his silk-web, at his shiny long table
Sipping at telephones, and his workers, caught,
Buzzing and gossiping

At the endless benches of their lives along which
The silk slid in thin rivers.

II

He liked bouncing in the bales, sneezing into
Their dusty canvas hides like crabby shells –
Lying outstretched over them

Gripping the cordage with one's hands
And one's feet braced, one's loins
Buried in some special penknifed silken gash, and one was

That male spider with a bellyful of silk oneself.
He would watch the canteen flies,
All possible silk, and at home

He kept in a pearly bottle choked with gossamer
A lustrous great spider he fly-fed; he had become
Clever enough to snatch them on the wing

Wondering at how the beautiful webs
Could yet be spun out of the corrupt glues
That were the fly's food; he mused upon

Those husks caught up in orrery rounds,
Emptied of all purpose, yet white
And winged as angels. He knew

The silk of his employment was spun by worms
Of a moth, and dreamed of feeding that moth
To his spider, the silk would be redistilled, radiant

With the light and pulsing beauty of all the trembling moths
That spin silk clothes for the babies of themselves
Wrapped and cross-clawed like an Egyptian Karast.

III

The butterfly or the sulphur-moth sucking at her weed
Is only one of the beauties; her transformation
To thin taut threads under the same sun on which the spider

Dances to eat her is another of them,
The skeletal patterns of cracked shadows in the sun;
And the beauty of the crabby lichen-back

That chucks her loins from side to side
Like Lola Montez, and tiptoes out
To wrap on tautened lines her prey in bales,

Is yet another, as he thinks
Drowsily of sleep, that great spider
Bending down to suck his soul from his face,

Kissing face to face, and turning it
Into that sensitive web which fills the nightworld
And catches fluttering dreams for nourishment;

So Renfield's madness or peculiarity
That loved the creatures so
The rest of us despise, led him

Fearlessly into the night of dreams,
Young silk-factor, where he met the master, Vlad,
Who fed him endlessly from thin soft hands.

IV

Who fed him endless streams of drops on wings
Like mother's milk, choice flies, and told him:
'Be that spider whom you fear, I, Vlad Dracula,

Will so transform you, as you wish,' and showed him how
Life flows in liquid drops, through fangs,
Creature to creature, in chains of drops like webs,

And whose work he did, so long as he was strong,
Guiding the young white girls to dance
Upon the webs without being caught by Death,

Raising them to drink as It did, spiderly,
Until fly-swatting Van Helsing clapped his fat palms
Smack and said 'No more of those,' wiping hands

Stained from the stake down immaculate spun hose.

ORCHARD WITH WASPS

The rouged fruits in
The orchard by the waterfall, the bronzed fruits,

The brassy flush on the apples.
He gripped the fruit

And it buzzed like a gong stilled with his fingers
And a wasp flew out with its note

From the gong of sugar and scented rain
All the gongs shining like big rain under the trees

Within the sound of the little waterfall
Like a gash in the apple-flesh of time

Streaming with its juices and bruised.
Such a wasp, so full of sugar

Flew out within the sound
Of the apple-scented waterfall,

Such a gondola of yellow rooms
Striped with black rooms

Fuelled with syrups hovering
At the point of crystal,

Applegenius, loverwasp, scimitar
Of scented air and sugar-energy

Shining up his lamp-tree tall and devious
Given utterly to its transformations

From sharp-scented flowers to honey-gongs,
Giver and taker of pollination-favours,

A small price for such syrups and plunderings,
Its barky flesh, its beckoning fruit,

Its deep odour of cider and withering grasses,
Its brassy bottles and its Aladdin gold-black drunks.

GUNS AND WELLS

The artillery-men wait upon the big gun,
They have its banquet piled
And ready in greased pyramids,
They serve the long fat shells like cannelloni,
The gun munches with an explosion.

Molten tears silver our countenances,
Vomit of metal plates the cornfields,
Men blow away like smoke in the ringing brisants.

No doing of mine, says chef-commandant,
I feed the guns only when they are hungry.

She tells me the polished skull of a traitor
Lurks in this well still,
His comrades gave rough justice,
Over the parapet laid his bare neck,
Cutlass-sliced that smuggling head,
Which dropped like a boulder
And is down there to this day, she said,

Polished nearly to nothing,
Bobbing in the well-spring,
Folding and unfolding in the polishing water,
Almost glass, and papery-thin,
Ascending, descending on variable cool water,
Nodding upon a current which is a spine,
Spinning like a film of faintest shadow
Or flexile churchwindow,
Reflating when rain fattens the spring;

Then a sunbeam
Strikes down the brick shaft
And there gazes upwards, revolving in the depths,
A golden face; then the sun

Goes in and the water goes on polishing.

THE WHITE, NIGHT-FLYING
MOTHS CALLED 'SOULS'

I

Their bodies all uncanny slime and light,
I brush silvery maggots off my white bible.

We are copies of each other. Bound in leather
The book crawls among us with a loud voice,

Dead men's matter wormed into chapters
Between the first communion doeskins.

Worms are the messengers rustling in the print with quills,
Masters of God's word, the bible bookworms;

We are dead men's matter, gene-edited,
Say God's bibles, covered with worms.

II

The moths flutter at the candles like clothed ladies,
Like long ladies in Assyrian gauzes;

The moonbeams twine through the flowers creating nectars,
The moths sip, and reclothe the moonbeams in light leathers

And dusty gauzes like Assyrians for their dances,
And these moonbeam moths sup at the candles

Like soft explosions.
The sunshine falls on meat, creating liquors

The blackflies sip
Dressing bright sun in greasy leathers,

Tight shining leathers, and like Assyrian dragons
Trample on my bible-hide and kneel roaring

At top pitch, dabbing with their suctions.
The little bony flies come to the Bible

Because it reeks of sacrifice. O God,
Burnt offerings like blue candles of the ghats

Twirl in smokes of fat to Your motionless courts,
And we brushed the stout Baal-zebub flies away

That wished to wing Your meat, and clothe it, God,
In white maggot-skin, like bibles. The Lord's talon

Out of thunder slashes meat, scorches off the skin
Like opening His book, and He snuffs the odour,

Clothing the meat-nectar in the Lord God; and Who
Brings His own untouched flesh to His pregnant Bride?

III

The wireless at midnight gives out its hum
Like a black fly of electricity, folded in wings.

A moth like a tiny lady dances to the set,
This hum is light to her, a boxed warm candle,

This set has inner gardens full of light.
Our baby, like a moth, flutters at its mother,

Who mutters to her baby, uttering milk
That dresses itself in white baby, who smiles

With milky creases up at the breast creating
Milky creases, and milk-hued water

Hangs in the sky, waiting for its clothes,
Like a great white ear floats over us, listening

To the mothy mother-mutter, or like a sky-beard smiles
And slips into its thunderous vestry and descends

In streaming sleeves of electrical arms
To run in gutters where it sucks and sings.

SONG

I chuck my Bible in the parlour fire.
The snake that lives behind the bars there
Sucks at the black book and sweats light;

As they burn together, the codex
Flips its pages over as if reading itself aloud
Memorising its own contents as it ascends curtseying

Like crowds of grey skirts in the chimney-lift,
In particles of soot like liberated print.
The vacant text glows white on pages that are black.

The stars, those illustrious watchers
Arranged in their picture-codes
With their clear heartbeats and their eager reading stares

Watch the guest ascend. Around us in the parlour
The inn-sign creaks like rowlocks.
The drinkers glower as my book burns,

Their brows look black
Like open books that turning thoughts consume.
Then all at once

With a gesture identical and simultaneous
Of reaching through the coat right into the heart
They all bring out their breast-pocket bibles

Like leather coals and pile them in the fire
And as they burn the men begin to sing
With voices sharp and warm as hearth-flames.

The black pads turn their gilded edges and
The winged stories of the angels rise
And all that remains is our gathering's will

Which assembles into song. Each man sings
Something that he has overheard, or learnt,
Some sing in tongues I do not understand,

But one man does not sing. I notice him
As my song takes me with the others. He is
Setting down the words in rapid shorthand

In a small fat pocketbook with gilded edges.

PHEROMONES

(Pheromones are 'external chemical messengers' given off by the body. They are said to communicate profound emotional and physiological effects from person to person.)

Dreaming of a dog, whose nostrils
Are his lightless eyes, means
Murder and riches; under the sunshine

Blazers bright as bluebells
With brass buttons yellow as butter;
The strong light

Shooting down the polished walking-sticks,
Running in sticks and streams,
Calls like trumpets

To the game;
The sea hedgehogged in gold,
Frogged in it, like a great blue blazer:

The great doorman with the labouring heart.
In this heat your scent is a snapshot,
Your spoor streams from you like a fragrant picture.

Your fingers
Sniff down your glass and walk into my lap.
It is so hot

My sex is a shelled snail,
And I excuse myself from You
For my nostrils wish to savour

The self-scent of my own sex
This gathering promotes,
And so my smelling fingers tremble first

At the eternal curry-smell of the brass handle
Of the metal of trumpets of the Gents
That it never loses or ever could lose;

Doubtless a dog would know its master
For over the brass in thinnest films are laid
The identities of all who have here touched themselves.

I bend my nose to the knob, for I swear
The champion of tennis employs this place;
I would know his sweat anywhere

After that magical game:
He filled the court with the odours of his perfect game,
Excellent musk, wiping his handle;

Let the trumpets call his prize!
I enter and am girded with personalities,
Long ghost snailing from the bowls

And gutters; my own genius mingles with that
Of the champion and the forty-seven assorted
Boozers I can distinguish here in silent music,

In odorous tapestries. In this Gents
We are creating a mingled
Essence of Gent whose powers

To the attuned nose
Are magnificent indeed
And shall affect the umpires

Who shall agree with what their noses
Tell them strides viewless from the urinal
Where the gentlemen sacrifice into stone bowls

In silent trance. Oh how
The tennis champion strikes pheromones
Under my guard with his far-sighted nose;

He has brought us to heat which calls him
In blond hair and buttons to his trumpeting prize.

THE GOLDEN POLICEMAN

She is today a combination of angel and doll.
Somehow she opens certain doors in the air.
The shell is warm and scented by the sun,

Rests in its light-fracturing sandbath among
The enormous shuffling nostrils of the dunes.
My skull is a creating gate, like the shell,

Echoing without question the sea's shuffling
Which is an excellence like touch.
There are little sandy spiders with their eyes

Gleaming like shoebuttons. There are
Granite boulders on our beaches,
And powder-puffs on her dressing-table.

The dew falls and crawls like the ghosts of spiders,
The waves come in like long cripples or snakes.
A policeman wonders about my reverie, which has

No visible means of support, until he looks round
And sees her too, salutes, and resumes his beat
Like the waves, policing.

His clothes are made of the shadowy look of misdoings,
His hickory truncheon of fines, his notebook
Of broken commandments. I stand by the dock of hulls

With this lady, and the sun breaks out of the clouds
Dusting him with gold, by some means
She has transformed the Law;

And I am very content, listening to the steel hulls
That ring like a run of bells to their riveters,
Like cathedrals made entirely of bell-metal,

Though the notes are low, very low, and listened to
By the soles of my feet more than my ears,
And beside the dock with its beached shells

The wind furrows roads through the sandy rushes.
The Law puts back its notebook, buttoning up his breast
With a golden stud stamped with her image, or

One like it; he has spoken a few words
Into his portable radio, which occupies his
Heartside, and he pauses to watch the water

Far out on the estuary patrolling
In its blue uniform. He looks like a projectile;
His helmet could be lined with stars

Like pricked velvet. As he tucks his notes away
New doors open and rush towards us across the ocean.

SILENCE FICTION

The late houses are built over the early caves,
The foundations and cellarage are where the first people lived.

We have fitted stout doors and hang their keys
High in the chimney-vaults where, out of sight,

They gather from the flames great swatches of soot,
Bunches of soot-flowers out of the food-fires,

Like the brushes of black foxes through the generations.
Then in the especial bad times a besmutched woman

Enters in defiled white to fetch down our keys
And open the earth to us. As she stands in the threshold

We know we must cast over our hearth pitchers of water,
And she treads through the warm ashes and with black sleeves

Reaches into the hanging soot,
Unhooks and rubs across her skirt revealing

The bright metal under the black grease. She
Throws the key down ringing on to the stone flags,

Leaves into the dusk for the next house.
We unlock and descend into the cellar-roots,

Light in the chimney-roots our lower fires,
And begin our lives on the unadorned earth floor

Some of which is sheer sand, elsewhere silky clay.
There we find shells of earliest cookery, and our fingertips

In the dirt encounter marvels of red-ochre bones,
Our torches tossing shadow like black potter's clay.

The wind blows through the upper houses, and the rain blows,
Cleansing hearth and porch, rinsing chimney. We know

By no messenger when to return; under the tangled
And matted hair, and the grime, and through the rags

That have rotted, a look shines,
An acceptance. Then we return

To the sunlit chimneys and the whitened hearths,
Out of the earth cradle; quenching the flares,

Troop chattering out of the cellar stairs,
Draw baths and strop to mirror-glass the rusty razors,

Secure the lower doors with their immense keys we hang
Shining bright in the chimneys; light our upper fires.

The black soot feathers through generations on the long keys.
We recall wondering, occasionally, that in those cellars

We never spoke, not at any time; once through the door
We were to keep and breath the silence

That had gathered there like foundation water
In the roots of the chattering houses, deep and pure.

CALL

for F.

The shipwright's beauty, who butchers the forest,
Dresses it again in shining sails,

Garments like blossom,

And nailed with new iron like budding grain,
With big ship-bosoms full of wonderful fruit
And men of unbelievable expertise
Of knowledge of the stars and sands;

You serve branching ocean routes
As though the whole sea were a sailing-tree
And the ships were blossom on it
Gliding slowly
On its world-embracing boughs
Transferring goodness and prosperity,

You give them yare names:
Ocean Moon, Tidesource,
And their travellers a berth of womb
In the big-belly blown along
By blinding blossom;

And others dig
And uncover the scarlet iron
And with fire forge sounding hulls and bells
And the great mines of iron feather on the waters,
The heaviest stone sails the wide seas,

Or in the dusty dry dock
Resounds to its remaking
As a cathedral calls out to its glad city to serve.

IN THE PHARMACY

for Wendy Taylor

A moth settled on the side of a bottle,
Covering its label, a marvel. The embroidered wings
Of the moth called Wood Leopard. It flutters off

And settles on another bottle. The label of this violet
Fluted container with the glass stopper reads
Lapis invisibilitatis: it would make you disappear.

The moth like a travelling label walks
From bottle to marble bottle with floury wings
Embracing each and tapping with fernleaf tongue

Sugared drops at neck and stopper,
Built like a fat rabbit with gaudy wings extracting
The essence of pharmacies, the compendium,

Staggering from jar to sculptured jar and sealing
Into capsules its own cogitatio,
Implicating in its eggs our explicit medicine.

And the draughts of invisibility, the poisons?
The caterpillar remembers to die, and disappears,
As the labelled stone declares,

All melts to caterpillar soup inside the wrappings
Where the pupa cogitates,
Just the nerve-cord floating like a herring-skeleton,

And round those nerves lovingly unfolds
The nervous wings on which is marked
In beautiful old pharmacy script, the formula.

THE HEART

An autumn bluebottle,
Frail winged husk with the last squeezings
Of the year sealed up inside,

The last juices and saps of the fruits
Crystallising inside the stone gaze
Of the insect-mask, countenance of sugars.

It sings softly, in search of sugars.
The maiden sings softly,
She whose red blouse

Is blowing on the line,
Its buttons glittering like sugar,
Full of the wind's tits,

That I saw her filling yesterday;
As though she had given one of her bodies
To the elements,

For the weather to fill,
The red blouse pulsing on the line,
Emptying and filling like a heart

In the strong gusts,
The wind's heart beating on the line;
And the sails of blood,

The stout red-rigged yachts competing on the estuary,
Red for celerity and heart,.
And the transparent word breathing everywhere.

The maiden and the fly sing softly,
It butts its drumstick head against her window,
She stares out at a heart of hers beating in the weather,

The fly so full of low sweetness it hums like rubbed crystal.

THE GREEN TOWER

(Carn Brae)

Leaves on their wooden shelves
Like shelf after shelf of shiny footgear
All marching on the wind,

Boots without soldiers,
The battleground of wind
Under one blue helmet,

Spirit soldiers marching in their winged boots,
The scyamore of the churchyard full of ghost
By this broad calm church

Light and airy and white with plain windows,
Built in the seventeen hundreds
Like a rational cabinet of light and praise

And at the nave-back a step down into an old tower,
The old bell-tower with the map of scores of churches
All the bell-able churches in Cornwall.

As I stepped down into this area
I thought that a high bell must still be ringing,
Have lately been rung,

Or its late echoes were caught still in the crystals
Of the dark stone blocks of this elder tower,
And like an electricity a slight

And relaxing current passed through my whole skin
And I stepped out into the broad church and there was nothing
And I stepped back into the stone tower that was tingling

And I stepped out and took her back down with me
And she felt it also, like the near presence of water.
And outside the tall tower was green from weather,

And with its gargoyles that looked like piskies of the rain,
Like a towering haunt of piskies, the green tower;
And every Sunday the tiger of blood

Lashed its tail on their altar,
The bible turned its pages
Over and over not wearing them out,

The souls all marched in the big
Thumping boots of their hymns,
The congregation roaring aloud with their cunning

Who have that sweet relenting pagan
Bell-hung current at their Cornish back.

KILLING HOUSE

Creates a haunted house
By filling it with dead folk; the church
A haunted killing-house of graves

That gathers all ghosts with its one death,
One continuous death
That has lasted roughly 2000 years so far,

The same death in all the churches simultaneously,
A death from which ghost issues ceaselessly.
There are rolling rivers

Of all the houseless secular ghosts
Like mists created by the dying leaves,
Like the white rivers of Par,

Like wooded hills that blow fanfares of ghosts
On the night wind as the moon rises.
It houses them.

II

God must be naked
Since we remove our clothes to create souls,
We pass the ghost shuddering from person to person

As one would hang an impossible suspension,
A perilous shaking bridge like the impossible thing
Everlastingly done in church,

Killing and eating the god that cannot die
Which creates much ghost;
And that other world breaks through

Crying in Christ's voice for Mama;
The women making themselves up and perfuming themselves,
Charging themselves with ghost,

Opening their naves,
Gardeners and flowers in one,
Haunted gardens of the future children

Who pluck as they arrive the red flowers.
An aeroplane scratches the high sky with steam;
Like a child in a haunted house

We rub the windowpane to catch a glimpse,
We desire to watch a thing which is not ghost.
If you are not baptised in church

God does not know your name
To call you unto Him,
It was not said out loud

Into his vaulted ear, and with this fright
They drive the ghosts back year after year
Woolbacks stiff with threat unto their shepherd

Before the Cross where unthinkable things occur,
The crossing of the wooden bridge
By the nails in it, the haunted

Bleeding footbridge dangling at nave's end.

THE QUIET WOMAN OF
CHANCERY LANE

The blind girl points at a star.
At night, she says, when all the stars are out,
She feels their rays feathering on her face,
Like a fringe of threads.

She stands by the beehive's low thunder.
There will be snow, the bees of ice
Will swarm from their darkening hives. I see

Clouds are gliding, and becoming, in the moonlight,
Mountaineering from nowhere, as the mass of air,
The town's hanging breath, soars into the cold
And is ice in dirigible bergs
And apparitions of a terrain they have created:
Cloudscape. How, under these glories, I wonder

Can men stroll past in deadblack suits, signifying
Ignorance and blindness of the skin,
Swinging griefcases packed with inky briefs,
And a spring in their step from this uniform?
They have a blind confidence, she says, in their power
And in the courts cry 'Proof, proof!',
They can make all others' skins go sightless,

Blind with worry, yet mine, she says,
The Quiet Woman without eyes,
Not living in my head,
The Headless Woman, my skin
Is open as the night sky, with the remote stars
And nearer glories easing across; my eyes
Are blind, but I know these people
By the no-shapes of their numbness as they go,
But since, blind, I am not in their power,
Being afflicted by God, they will not touch me,

With their penal pleading, for I belong
To Another, Who has my eyes. These lawful men
To her are like stars that have gone black, turned
Inside out with the suction of nothingness,
Empty sockets walking the Inns of Court.

The blind girl points to the stars
As if she could see; she informs me
How a special breath from space
Tells her they are out in their moist fullness.
Yet the sky is so packed, how can she not,
Pointing, light on some constellation or other?

But I believe her when she tells me how
Her life without eyes is so full. I take
The blind girl by her night hand.
With her fingers raised, she traces in the air
The slow rising of that mountain that hangs, the full moon,

It is like the presence of a fountain, she says,
Like the fresh aura of falling water, or like
That full head of the thistle I stroked in the park,
And its sound is like a fountain too, or like snow thistling.

UNDER THE DUVET

Sleep-feather, the sleep-feather
Comes drifting down,
Rocking the child to sleep,

The child sleeps covered
In a bag of drifting sleep-feathers;
Eider-plume, the ducks are flying

Loftily through feathered clouds.
She sleeps flying through their death,
Their flow of plumage, bag of the whole flock.

Just as we realise with care
That we are dreaming, just there,
Entering the Self, and leaving, just there,

That we are asleep, and watching a dream,
And just there, waking, but entering
The small door of a second, the opening of a tick,

The nip of a cog, and watching,
Our Mother above shakes out her bag and the snow flies,
Or the dew manifests, like stars

They are suddenly there, a multitudinising of the grasses,
A heavying and a lighting-up,
We glance down, and the dew is there,

Like all the still seconds
There ever were, stopped,
Each one seeing into the morning, deep

In the interior of its glance, the morning;
And it is a dream of feathery embrace
Like a cloud pluming a mountain,

And the fleeces of sheep too heavy to walk,
So they must settle, and sleep
As the cloud settles

Grazing the mountain, among the silvered grass
Where all, air, mountain, sheep
Is a feathered being, silent with fog,

And within a fleeced pinion
I see the dark mouth of a cave
And enter the cavern

And am immediately among
A feathering of echoes
And I remember that Goddess

Who hid her child to conceal his cries,
Hid him in a cave known for winding passages
And galleries among which the echoes

Never ceased to cry, and surely
This is the passage along which the cloud retires
To its mountain's interior in the daytime,

To its inner pasture, and I find
That my hair and my dress
Are plumed with that cloud's dew

As the spiderwebs and the grasses are feathered
On every fibre with the water
Of the mountain's grey brain ever-distilling

Among its cool granite convolutions
And I squeeze droplets out of my sleeve
On to my lips, the cloth is rough and the taste

Is of cloth, sheep, grass, wings and ancient water
Stilled over and redistilled until it shines
Again like the plumage

Birthwet from its egg of the newborn angel.

CORNWALL HONEYMOON

Kaolin. A white shadow
Spread across half a county. All the streams
Flaming white. The soil packed

Underfoot solid with light. A beach
With drifts of dead leaves instead of pebbles.
Flowering fogs and the cold fur of moths.

The waves curl and dry,
Leave lines of tiny shells, the fruits
Of the spent waves. After the bath

She blazed with beauty. The crane of the docks
Like a fire-escape to heaven, a staircase
Of steel into the sky, I will see it

Magnificently wreathed in ivy. The eyes
Meeting in orgasm, the salty breath exchanged,
The kaolin waters of the man and woman mingling,

They have ascended the wreathed staircase completely.

SHELLS

See shells only as seawater twining back
To the first touch, of seawater on itself;

The water touching itself in a certain way,
With a certain recoil and return, and the mollusc

Starts up in the water, as though the conched wave
Had been struck to stone, yet with the touch

Still enrolled in it, the spot was struck
And life flooded through it

Recording a thin stone pulse of itself,
Its spiral photo-album, its family likeness

Caught in nacreous layers, as if
Your skull grew spiring from a skull-button,

Your roles coiling out of your smallest beginning,
Full of shelves of selves

Turning around each other
Like a white library that has been twisted,

Like a spired library turned in the tornado
Unharmed, keeping the well of itself

Open to past and future,
Full, like the mollusc, of the meat of sense,

The briny meat, twirled by the tornado;
And this, whose fleshy books have swum away,

Emptying the magnificent pearl-building,
All its walls luminous in the sunlight,

Empty stairwell full of sound,
For since the books created the shelves

To fit their message and their likeness,
Echoes of books remain, resounding,

Printed endlessly around the shelving,
Like the seasound of seapages turning over

And over, touching themselves
In a certain way, echoing, reminding,

Evoking new themes of old sea-shapes. A new shell,
A new skull begins again from its speck

Echoing the older books made of water.
See how the clouds coil also above the eggshells of cities,

Touching each other in certain ways, so that
Rain falls; clouds invisible

Over the sea, but when the watery air
Lifts over the land, the white shells float

Crystallised over the hot cities, muttering with thunder.

THE PROPER HALO

In those glad days when I had hair,
I used to love to smarm it down with Brylcreem.
In those old days this was the definition of a boy:
A scowl, Brylcreem, and back pockets, admonished
To refrain from pomades at one's confirmation,
So that the Bishop would not get his hands oiled,
Greasy palms, laying them on. My uncle laughed at me,
And called me 'Horace!' with my flat-combed parting,
My head shining like a boot; though, as a Navy man,
He liked all that sort of thing himself,
Shaking a kind of Bay Rum out of a nozzled bottle
Labelled in Arabic that came from Egypt,
A brick-red Sphinx on yellow sand for scene,
Spidered with Arabic like uncombed hair. Retired,
He would send to London to the importers for it,
And I asked him what the spider-writing meant. He told me:
'If you want to be like Horace, employ our oil.'

When he died, he left me his personal things,
A wristwatch with a back pitted
From tropical sweat, studs and cufflinks
Glorified with tiny diamond-chips, a dressing-case
With hairbrushes useful to me then, his shaving-mirror;
I mourned him, but enjoyed using his things,
Conversing with his shade, taking both parts in the mirror,
Remembering how we talked, fascinated by this grown-up;
And I remembered catching the habit of hairgrease,
He dropping a little in my palm and showing me
How to rub it in with fingertips, 'You'll
Never lose it now, keep up the massage,'
Which wasn't true. Still, when he died
I did have hair, and liked the barber's shop.

A university friend staying with me
Translated the Arabic on the bottle,
Laughing. I said '*What* spirit?' and he said
'Definitely religious advertising; could your uncle
Read the Arabic?' I thought not, though he had
Many spoken phrases. 'Then he picked up "Horace"
From the vendor's gabble; it reads:
"Horus comes to greet you through this oil." '

I liked the barber's shop; the man
Stabs the pointed bottle at his palm;
My dark hair is cut and shaped and forests felled
Over my white-sheathed shoulders lie like toppled pines.
The oil shivers in the barber's palm,
He puts the plump bottle down, and that hand
Descends swooping on the other; they rub together
Like mating birds and as they fly to my head
I see they shine. His rough fingertips
Massage my scalp like the beating of a flock
Of doves; now it is my hair that shines
And stands up as though an ecclesiastical charge
Were passing through me; I laugh! 'You like
The scent of the oil, do you, Sir?' I nod,
Though I don't. It's the shine I love;
I shine with glory! and this is worth
The barber's shillings, many times. I shall feel
Of age as down the street I pass
In my shining pelt and glittering shako, my hair
Cut and shaped like my natural urges, properly, proudly,
In a halo of light and scent, godly contained.

THE FUNERAL

for N.

I

Clouds and mountains were invited, both the conscious
And the unconscious creatures. The trees
Like visible outpourings of the stream's music,
The urine of the animals in the dawn frost
Puffing like rifle-fire. The dark meat of the sun,
The bloody meat, the cremating sun.

II

Ninety-two percent of what we eat is from direct
Pollination by the bees, he tells me this
To cheer me and if true ninety-two percent
Of what he says with his mouth is said by bees. The first light
On leaves shines like apples hanging in the trees,
The whole forest a vast orchard, and all things
Are more than they seem, for they may fly away,
And disappear like Mother pausing on the threshold
Of the fields of light, which are like dew
Thick in the grassy meadows, for the light hangs
Dripping in the leaves, stands on the wind.

III

There is a Witness, I think, who has magnetic wings.
First it seemed to me at the funeral service with the terrible
Useless brass handles that would be saved screwed to
The veneer cardboard coffin which was much too small
That my emotions such as these swirled round my flesh
And some of them spurted from my eyes but ninety-two
                                        percent

Were beating in my back in a sensation like spread wings.
Since mine were sprouting I was able to see
The wings of others, such as my father's, standing next to me,
And his were ragged and tattered like those of an old moth
Close to drying up and drifting away, it seemed my duty
To merge my birth-wet wings with his, and this I did,
Entwining them in an embrace with him that he would never
                                                    know,

And sure enough he, the widower, perked up,
And I felt tattered, but not dry, for back at the house
I sobbed my heart out in the little white-tiled loo,
And there was still a little angelic witness lodged in my spine
At the small of my back, in Jesus-robes, little calm watcher
In white, which I cannot explain, merely report.

                              I V

The other thing the funeral showed me, unpromising seance,
My Mother, subject of it, at the door ajar
On the field of light, looking back over her shoulder,
Smiling happiness and blessing me, the coherent veil
Of the radiant field humming with bees that lapped the water,
                                                    and she bent
And washed her tired face away with dew and became a spirit.

I

Death as pure loss, or immutability.
A watch falling into the well,
Ticking a while in the cool spring, distributing

Its faint shock; or death
As a diamond-second in the year, set
Glittering cold in the anniversary,

The tiny diamond in her ear
Surviving the cremation?

II

Death suddenly appearing, like a spiderweb in the fog,
A piece of paper opening into a house, the snapshot
Through an open door, and at the table sitting still

Somebody; the house
With one room and no kitchen,
The house with the card door;

The disposable house.

III

I turn my back on the ascensions,
The unscreened smokestacks, I do not wish
To watch her ascending, the knots

Solving themselves, fading,
Climbing into the antechambers of rain.
Besides, her smoke should be white,

Blinding!

And the colour of lost rain escaping!
And the photographs white
As the clothes are empty.

I open the prayer-book;
It is empty.

So, with her death,
I will baptise this small
Quartz; it shall stand for death

Like a glass room
Of which only a spirit knows the door,

Which only a spirit can enter
Turning and showing itself in the walls
Lined with warm mirror

Knowing its form in floor and ceiling,
Able to say 'I am here!'

v

It shall become a custom,
Warm room ringed to my finger,
Warm so long as I am warm,
Then left to my daughter

To keep warm, and bequeathed
To hers; warm stone
It will house multitudes.

TRANSACTIONS

I

The waves break on the shore with a scent
Of briny cellars of sea-fungus shrouding
Drowned shiny forests. I have a white door
To my cellar which when I crack open
Is as though the house were a wave, stopped,
Overhanging, and in the still
Round cellar in that moment's time
The mushrooms manifested. I put them there.
A pulse of phosphorescence keeps the house up.

II

The little mushrooms are salt
And they smell of zest and venom.
I swim into the yesty air of the cellar
And see them stand like white circular messengers,
Helicopter-winged angels.
Stiff one-vertebra spine.

III

The pylons choiring in the wind
Marching like the X-rays of cathedrals
Along their zesty ozone spoor like the odour of mushrooms,
The earth spinning within its mother, the waters,
Around its father, the sun,
Within clear sight of its godmother,
The mob-capped, nectar-rayed moon.

Whose white patched cap resembles a mushroom
Flying in its helicopter wings of magnetism
That raise the metal-sheeted tides
And crack them open scenting the sea-air with zest,
The pylons choiring,
Her silvery blouse flashing with electricity
Through its opening leaking her ozones
As the moonbeams scent the night-opening flowers,
My white shirt like an electric ghost
Specially laundered to enter this darkness
Under the cellar stairs where the white door stands open.

LIGHTS IN THE MIST

Lights in the mist branching across the water
Like fruit shining out of an orchard.
Then the mist clears, and the waves are disclosed
Stacked to the horizon, each with its poised sound,
Visible sound.

Her sleeping glances, her sleeping gloves,
Her body like some soft delectable debris
Awaiting collection. He breathed her odour in,
The carelessness of her relaxation overcame him
As no planned seduction could. He tastes the apple
She was eating when he began touching her.
The explosions of sea on the walls,
Random shell-bursts, traversing. Now she dreams

Of putting the final touches to the firstborn,
Knitting the baby's only garment with bone needles,
Engraving on the flesh the fingerprints like a colophon.

Dewy cobweb frozen like bone-of-lace; the orchard
Doing its one thing: creating leaves and fertilising flowers
And rounding fruit;

The water of the well twisting back into its brick socket.

Tasting alternately the cold earthy water, and the cool
Earthy fruits out of the apple-tree rooted in the wall.

The fenestral mists branching. The new veins branching.

THE MAN NAMED EAST

The dew, the healing dew, that appears
Like the dream, without warning, hovering on the blades;
The motions of his wings bring dew and light,

The man named East. The ghosts have lost
All sense of perspective
In the drinking-water, twisting and turning,

Shaped by too many vessels, and furrowed
By too many fearful vessels, for we
Drink the water of a drowned village

Of a drowned College from College Reservoir,
And across our drinking-water goes
A small yacht like a lighted kitchen,

A fishing-boat like a ruined cottage,
Dinghies like little violins
With squeaky rowlocks, with violin-voices,

With the devil's music written on the waters.
I stand by the small stream which contributes.
I kneel and dip my hand in, it insists

Into my palm with a slight pressure
Like a baby's hand, which is still
The elasticity of yards of water

Reaching down the hill
From the clouds on high; I crouch
With my hand in that baby's hand

Feeling the slight movement of its fingers,
The light clasp which is love,
The little bony stones rattle

And the cool flesh of glass sinews;
It babbles like a baby, I bend
My ear to the water and now I find

Underspeech I did not hear before;
With the forest like a vast moth
Settling its wings on the hill,

I dip my finger in my mouth and taste
Forests and air and the ice
Of the white rain-wing and its power-pinions.

MOTHERS AND CHILD

I

The soft modelling for hours,
The soft handling.
Undressing, she forgets to say her prayers.

The town of wives, promenading,
Staring among the lighted beauty-shops
Which are shadows of the beauty that is above,

That is too bright to look at
Except in the shadowing of lipstick and powder,
Painting with colour, camera obscura,

This in the town of the two electricities,
The powerhouse, lighting the shops,
The wives, stiff in their orgasms

With fingers stretched like starfish
And eyes going like electric bulbs,
Witch-hair cracking the taut white pillow;

And the stiff filamentous reach of the powerstation
Incandescent also in its circuits
Like some miraculous gestating glow-worm

Or silk-spinner of tungsten
That shines with that power,
The elastic of magnetism,

For whirl wheel within wheel
It comes spitting
Into the lamps, over the sheets

Of the great metropolis of rooms
And the lighted villages of wives
With the lover wanting the skin off

Wanting the electricity in essence,
The stripped wires,
Electricity with its rubber off,

Electricity more naked than last time;
He strokes for hours
Mowing the magnetism,

The sheets crackling,
The soft handling over and over,
And gradually the first skins loosen;

And the wives observe this recreation
As the mother her rounding belly
And wishes her child to be naked of it

Herself now willing her own birth
As the fish skips out of the wave
To be nude of the water

Water that peels off water as it marches
Nakedness off salt nakedness,
So that, undressing, she forgets to say her prayers,

As water forgets, and reflects
The beauty above her.

II

Or does she beam beauty up
To be bounced off the ceiling
Or off the man above her,

Transforming her beauty
Into his (and he needs it);
Her fighting-gear

A silk shirt,
Excellent accumulator of electricities,
Admirable rubbing battery of orgasms,

Or, as they say, Static,
For time stands still.
Such heroes as there might be

Awake when they touch her skin,
With a silent shout of recognition,
Skin which flutters unbearably

When they touch it sufficiently,
Like a moth beating in the light of the sheets,
The moth whose wings are flaming

Without being consumed;
And the wellspring where the more it is drawn
The more it flows;

While the wife as mother of herself opens
And draws herself off
That which steps out

Over the sill, the berth, the landing-place.

DRINK TO THE DUKE

The Duke of Burgundy, who represents
The drunkenness of battle,
With the deep purple of its soldiers,
Those bottles of hot blood
Caved in immense tuns
Under the battle-field, bottlefield,
Where it travels with its iron into the grapes;
Burgundy, you are drinking soldiers,
And have always done so –

And the Duke in his iron rage,
His moustache erect, his eyes bolting,
Reining his horse so she stands
Huge on her hind legs,
And the great insect carapace leaning sideways
With its white eyes in the coal-scuttle helmet
Glaring like the soul of a mantis,
And the noble sword scything down,
Uncorking you, drinking you by the neck.

LEGIBLE HOURS

The legibility of the evening,
The union of grapes,
We drink it and its spiritous consummation
In this brandy that shines in the dark within,
With the lamps blowing,
The flames like enraged tigers
Roaring in their thin glittering cages,
Ravenous oil-eaters.

The stinking shadows fly out of the wooden windows.
In the dawn, the brittle machine of salt,
The salt bread of the sea, fish for breakfast,
Feathery skeleton, pinion of the sea;
On the smooth-spun sand
Imprint of constellations,
Starcast of the brine, starfish.

Then the evening made legible
By the recording of a ghost
Or an opera of ghosts, the impress,
The mediumistic conches attending, the ear-shells,
The ghost's whorls spinning in their skirts,
Her contractions and ululations,
Her abyssing to her still axle,
Her repeats, her expansion
To the night sky, circling,
The display and occultation
On the night air of her grave that turns.

The legibility of the house.
The courtyard tree,
Green harbour of ten thousand ships
Tending anchor, optical toy of deep shade;

Can you hear the light hum circling in echoes
Around the stream, and the reflections
Caught in the woods and the inextricable shadows
All combing one way, can you? and there!
As the tide turns the weir-sound changes
Its pictures and the tree-head lightens
In the legibility of the grape and the new morning.

PNEUMONIA BLOUSES

The iron ships come in with hellish music
They are dedicated to golden oils and engines
And explosive riveting, their hulls heal
To tattoos of guns or iron drums, riveting.
And they worship the horse-mackerel and the sardine,
And why not, it is a living,
And a multitudinous beauty, that brings the souls in.
You see the machine-shop glitter in the tin,
They are water-moths flocking in their thousands;
The packers fit the silver engines in
Laid down in olive oil that is golden;
The key unwinds. Girls
In pneumonia blouses greet the fishermen
Whose balls are brimmed with nitroglycerine of souls,
In each lacy belly the embryo buoyant
As a nenuphar. In the sunlight
The old stone watches sweet and yellow as honeycomb.
Holding the milky child
Is like holding sleep in a bundle,
Which seeps everywhere. There is still frost
In the early morning shadows like spirit-photographs
And like the lace of girls in pneumonia blouses
Ruffled as are the wakes of working boats, fishermen's eyes
Open in all directions, but the shadow of night
Trawl them back again, the nets
Invisible in the black water.

HORSE LOOKING OVER
DRYSTONE WALL

_____

for S.C.

A horse dips his nose into dry shadow
Gathered in the chinks like water.
He drinks the coastal dark
That dwells behind the wallstones
in the dry boulder caverns.

Light lies along his muzzle like a stone sheath.
From skull-darkness kin to the dry stone wall
The eyes watch like mirrors of stone;
This horse is half light, half dark,
Half flesh and half stone
Resting his silver muzzle on the shadowed wall
Like a horse made partly of the silver of clouds,

And partly it is a boulder with mane and nostrils
Watching over his wall the plentiful wild boulders
Maned with shaggy weed in galloping water which are kin,

Coralled boulders nostrilling under their manes and
                                    lathered with brine.

BELLS

Bells, the men are mending
The broken church-bells
In the silent church
Silent as a hollow cliff,
They clamber in linen-covered boots
Up and down the bells' mountains,
The chafing of their clambering boots
Produces from all the bells
A low sweet humming,
From the serious shape of bells
Their sound-look of sorrow
Like a tear swinging and crying
Crying and never falling;
The church with its note
That must be charged by bells,
Nave-tone that gathers
Gradually into audibility
Like a singing, and falls
Below the threshold of hearing

Unless it is rung and charged
By bells with true notes
And men with the changes right;
That prolongs the singing.
The men are repairing them.
Buds like birds sit perched
With tightly-folded wings,
The bush is like a silent church
Ready to sound.
In the cliff a great door of sunshine
Swings open and closes again
As the clouds scud: ice-grey chalk
Flooding with gold.

It is full of tuned chambers that are tiny shells
With ancient frosty tones, it is a milliard church,
And a flood-lit skull that goes dark;
A chalkface mirror
To sunshine, like a moon on earth; the child
Stands a moment in its light
And walks away inspired;
In the sun's heat
The crystals of chalk, the tiny fossils
In their billions
Have given off a tone
Like a bell mended by the sunlight.
The quarry nearby
Bears the open wound of the church
Ripped from its flank, in negative.

IN THE HALL OF
THE SAURIANS

In the Hall of Saurians, the light worked the bones,
The shadows stamped. I was haunted
With the heads colossal in death.
My father brought me here
In his bright shadowless car,
His jewel which he drives everywhere
As a coffin is lined in white satin
Brilliant in the darkness, like mother of pearl.

The wall of the Insect Gallery is spashed
In a butterfly shape with all the British Lepidoptera
And there are five times as many moths shown
For the Shadow in these times
Is correspondingly more significant than the Light.
What goes on in the darkness sees by perfume.
They say that to go out in the noon
Is to lose one's shadow,
To lose the moth of onself.

My seed, my moth, was torn from me
Like gossamer in the wind
By the lady curator of all these bones,
Mistress of the Halls of Patterns of Death,
Keeper of the probable forms,
The underworld that is delivering constantly
The forms of life, at night like mud
That is a turreted museum, with endless galleries,
But at dawn, nevertheless,
The rainbow glides closer to us across the water
Until we stand within its coloured shells,
Its sequent halls. This is our form
Of transport, the ecstasy of these halls,

The forms displayed. My father in his jewel
Scurries away among the beetles.
The corpse of London transforms in his mouth,
His tales make of it a winged thing
Full of custom and surprise.
But these are winged buildings
As we make love after hours
In the Hall of the Saurians, and the flickering light
Works the bones and the shadows stomp
As up to a campfire smoky with jungle moths
To warm themselves or crush it out.

A FEW CARATS OF PAIN

The shadows were roaring
With pain on the other side of the mirror,
She pushed the glass up against the optic
But called the barman to draw my beer;
'You lose your grip,' she said,
'In rheumatoid arthritis, which is
Stone in the garden of the joints,'
She explained, and in the east wind
As if ice in the air were condensing on this stone,
Black ice; 'Verglas?' She agreed.

Welding in the glass,
Immovable joints under construction,
On the other side of the mirror
Shadows arced out on her face.
She served me chaser whisky anodyne
And the barman drew my beer in his firm grip.
'That's a handsome stone, my dear . . .'
'It's my life-savings, lover-boy,
Small as it is . . .' among the calcite flowers
Like an arc-tooth in the garden, refracting pain;
'You lost your grip at first
And no sign can be seen except the pain,
So I bought the diamond
To wear on my arthritic hand.' It was like
A folded window into the skin,
It was like a point of pain
Held on a gold band of concentration,
Its interior shadowless.

Her hand, she says, is a garden to this star
Which is a precipice when the east wind blows
And you lose your grip; you know your bones

In this disease, she says, outlined by pain,
'I've crowned this one like a King
With my life-savings . . .' she pushed
My glass up into the whisky-spring, and smiled;
Her perfume filled the bar, her story gripped us.

AT THE COSH-SHOP

Hard rubber in its silk sheath like a nightie:
The assistant offered me a small equaliser,

A Soho Lawyer that could be holstered
In a specially-tailored back pocket,

And he would introduce me to his friend
The trouser-maker. I did not think this

Necessary, but I asked, Why the silk?
It seemed luxurious for such a hard argument.

Oh, Sir, so that it will draw no blood!
He seemed surprised I asked; I thought this not right;

I believe it was the blackness
The makers did not like to show,

Like an executioner it should draw on
Lily gloves, or like a catering waiter

For an instrument that performs a religious service,
Letting the ghost our temporarily with a shriek:

While all is peace within
They steal your worldly goods

Settling the argument by appeal
To deep non-consciousness

With a swift side-swipe, the Bejasus out of him –
Or an act of sexuality, equivalent?

Do the same people make the instrument
That will put the Bejasus back into a person?

The silk then would be the finest, for silk chafing
Hard rubber rouses electricity, it would be

Moulded to the individual sculpt of her lover,
Providing wisely for a longish trip, could seem

Dressed in his silk pyjamas, hard and tingling,
Or as the white silky cloud conceals the thunder

And the black current
That is going to shoot its white darts up and through.

INTO THE ROTHKO
INSTALLATION

(Tate Gallery, London)

Dipping into the Tate
As with the bucket of oneself into a well
Of colour and odour, to smell the pictures
And the people steaming in front of the pictures,
To sniff up the odours of the colours, which are
The fragrances of people excited by the pictures;
As the paid walk down the gallery
On each side of them the Turners glow
As though they both were carrying radiance
In a lantern whose rays filled the hall like wings
That brushed the images, which glowed;

Into the Installation, which smells
Of lacquered canvas soaking up all fragrance,
Of cold stone, and her scent falters
Like cloth torn in front of the Rothkos
Which are the after-images of a door slammed
So blinding-white the artist must shut his eyes
And paint the colours floating in his darkness.

He chose the darkest of the images for that white,
That green; red on red beating to the point
Where the eye gasps, and gives up its perfume
Like a night-flowering plant; and with many
Thin washes he achieves the effect
Of a hidden light source which smells
Like water far off in the night, the eye
So parched; paintings you almost can't see;

As if in painting
The Israelites crossing the Red Sea
He painted the whole wall red, and,
Black on black therein,
God somewhat like a lintel. We brought
The lanterns of ourselves in here
And your imagination blotted our light up, Rothko;
The black reached out, quenching our perfume
As in a dark chapel, dark with torn pall,
And our eyes were lead, sinking
Into that darkness all humans have for company;

Standing there, eyes wide, her lids faltered
And closed, and 'I see it, now' she said
And in her breath a wonderful blaze
Of colour of her self-smell
Where she saw that spirit-brightness
Of a door slammed open, and a certain green insertion
Shifting as her gaze searched
What seemed like a meadow through the white door
Made of lightning, cloud or flowers, like Venusberg
Opening white portals in the green mountain
Stuffed with light, he having used
The darkest of all that spectrum almost to blindness

And in his studio in the thin chalk of dawn
Having passed inwardly through that blackness,
Slitting his wrists, by process of red on red
He entered the chapel under the haunted mound
Where the white lightning of another world
Flashed, and built pillars. We left
The gallery of pictures rocked
By the perfume of a slammed eye, its corridors
Were wreathed with the detonation of all its pictures
In the quick of the eye, delighting into
Perfumes like fresh halls of crowded festival.

PLAYING DEAD

His dead–white face,
The eyelids of chalk
With the bold black cross marked

Cancelling the eyes, declaring
Hollow-socketed death, and the
Marble-white countenance

Declaring death
And the red nose to admit
He had died drinking

And the vertical eyelid-stripe
Telling us not only can he open
His eyes up and down but also

From side to side in the stare
Of a real ghost
Who does as he likes

Because Death breaks all the rules, and is
At very best an outrageous joke, and almost
Whatever Death does is quite soon forgotten;

So the Clown pratfalls on the skeleton
Of a banana, and two well-dressed Clowns
Accelerate with custard pies their mutual putrefaction,

As if it were funny to worry overmuch
About these bodies we wear like increasingly
Baggy pants with enormous knucklebuttons, especially
If like that sepulchral makeup they wipe off
In cold cream to white sheer speechless laughter.

A LOVER

to M.

Heavy magic sobs. They take omens
From the children's shouts playing near the Church.
The funeral is a way of preventing the formation

Of a lingering ghost. Stars
Linking down into the water
Among the lights of boats. Lift the Hare

And its fur is full of colour, it scurries
Through heath fires to confuse the scent.
She dazzled him with her blouse, dandled

Him in the bosom of it, the swooping front.
He thought he heard
Heavy magic sobs inside, from the heavy breasts

That swung as she walked, like two animals
Impassioned, trying to escape; her sweet smile
Above. She offered him

The whisky bottle, the shadowed bottle
Of dark glass. He felt the wells
Of friendship rising towards her, and they drank

Their dark spirit among the shadowed nettles,
Their waxes and poisonous greases. The children's shouts
Came floating over the common grass, which looked

Dusty and stale, as if it had not slept.
This is what it was like at Lodestone, with my grannie
Who was my parents, the stars linking down

Into the water, the hilly meadows
Where the hares box, where they
Dazzle us with everything created, outside

My grannie's dark kitchen, the houses
Standing open to the world, the hares boxing
On a thousand hills. She had a voice

Like a house, capacious, and with many
Cupboards, under the five-fingered stars,
And a blouse in which the breasts dazzled and boxed.

THE MOONS OF SCILLY

For S.C.

Grounded moons, a scrapheap
Of discarded moons, every one a beauty.
Sealed stone boilers of seaweed machines,
The stones that power the boiling spume-engines,
They are pulled by their great fellow-stone

In the sky that swoops low
And clocks them together,
That pulls the waves up against the cliffs
In great momentary ferns
And sends the shocks deep into their hearts

Where pictures form that glow for ages.

The cliffs are full of such pictures
Packed like recordings of these shaped shocks,
Millennial libraries of stone audios.

But you'd not know it from this stillness
In a palm-of-the-hand stone-meadow beach.
The sky is made of stone also.
There are many cracks in this palm from hard labour,
Turning the sea over and over;

The cracks in the stones are so deep
They look like iron straps. The shadows from the sky
Lie on the land so hard they deepen into cracks,
A palm seamed by slow action.

Some thunder-lizards retiring from time
Have become their eggs again.
They have rolled themselves up into their crocodilian
                                                    beginnings.

This shore is the skin of an egg too big to see.

The sands of all the deserts have formed into one single
                                                    fractured grain.

There are many broken stone torsos.
There is a great sphinx of rucked stone and closed eyes.

Lichens open like little scrolls all over its stone lids,
Lichen-books, library of sea-shocks, cloud-bursts.

And a wrecked boat on a stone foreshore becoming stone;
It has been there so long it has caught stone,
Infectious whiteness, deeply gorgonised,
The ground of pebbles its unyielding ocean.

THE BIG SLEEP

Sea, great sleepy
Syrup easing round the point, toiling
In two dials, like cogs

Of an immense sea-clock,
One roping in, the other out.
Salt honey, restless in its comb,

Ever-living, moving, salt sleep,
Sandy like the grains at eyes' corners
Of waking, or sleepiness, or ever-sleeping;

And when the sun shines, visited as by bees
Of the sun that glitter, and hum in every wave,
As though the honey collected the bees;

The honey that was before all flowers, sleepiness,
Deep gulfs of it, more of it than anything,
Except sleepy warm rock in the earth centre

Turning over slowly, creating magnetism,
Which is a kind of sleepiness, drowsy glue
Binding the fingers, weakly waking fingers,

Or fingers twitching lightly with the tides;
And the giant clock glides like portals, tics
Like eyelids of giants sleeping, and we lie

In Falmouth like many in a bed,
And when the big one turns
We all turn; some of us

Fall out of bed into the deep soil,
Our bones twitch to the tides,
Laid in their magnetic pattern, our waters

Rise like white spirits distilled by the moon,
Can get no further, and turn over
Heavy as honey into the sea

To sleep and dream, and when the big one dreams
We all dream. And when she storms
We all weep and ache, and some fall

Into her gulfs as she tosses, and we weep
For the lifeboats toiling on the nightmares . . .
But in those beds waters touch each other

Coiling, in a certain way, and where they touch,
At the very point, a mineral spark,
A bone begins to grow, someone is

Putting bones together in the gulf,
In her accustomed patterns – and in their season
The women walk about the town, a big drop

Of the Dreamer in their bellies, and in the drop
A smaller dreamer, image of themselves,
Who are the image dreamed by the ocean's drop,

By the two clocks, one roping in, one out.